D1268292

THE COMPLETE
BASENJI

ELSPET FORD

New York

Maxwell Macmillan Canada
Toronto

Maxwell Macmillan International
New York Oxford Singapore Sydney

Copyright © 1993 by Elspet Ford

Howell Book House
Macmillan Publishing Company
866 Third Avenue
New York, NY 10022

Maxwell Macmillan Canada, Inc.
1200 Eglinton Avenue East
Suite 200
Don Mills, Ontario M3C 3N1

Macmillan Publishing Company is part of the Maxwell Communication Group of Companies.

Library of Congress Cataloging-in-Publication Data

Ford, Elspet.
    The complete Basenji / Elspet Ford.
            p.   cm.
        ISBN 0-87605-016-X
        1. Basenji. I. Title.
SF429.B15F67 1993
636.7'53–dc20   92-31091
                                                     CIP

Macmillan books are available at special discounts for bulk purchases for sales promotions, premiums, fund-raising, or educational use. For details, contact:

Special Sales Director
Macmillan Publishing Company
866 Third Avenue
New York, NY 10022

10 9 8 7 6 5 4 3 2 1
Printed and bound in Singapore

CONTENTS

THE BASENJI

B is for Barkless, but not really mute.
   They chortle and yodel, mutter and growl
   I think they could talk if they ever learnt how.
A is for Agile, graceful and quick.
   They jump like a deer and play like a cat.
   Who ever heard of a dog acting like that?
S is for Stubborn, yes they do have a streak.
   They'll coax and they'll bully till they get their own way.
   Outsmarting a human is just part of their day.
E is for Entertaining, they're all hams at heart.
   Ask them to play and they'll act like a clown.
   Tell them to heel and they'll sit down and frown.
N is for Neat, a must in themselves.
   They lick and they groom till each hair is in place.
   If they think that you need it, they'll come wash your face.
J is for Jungle, natives and huts.
   On the tombs of the Pharoahs their pictures are found,
   And in Africa's jungles they're the belled hunting hound.
I is for Me. An owner possessed,
   I feed and I doctor, I worry and care.
   And that doggone Basenji knows, when he calls, I'll be there.

Jeraldeen Crandall. 1967

ACKNOWLEDGEMENTS

The love and interest aroused by a little prick-eared curly-tailed dog from Africa with the mentality of a mischievous clown has allowed me and many others to make friends worldwide. These friends and the writings of Basenji lovers of previous years have helped me compile this book, to weave the story of the Basenji, both in and out of Africa, into a coherent whole. It is not really my book – it belongs to all who were, and are, fascinated by the Basenji and its history. Because that history in the modern world is still within living memory, it has been possible to check statements, and fallacies, and to bring together in one volume a story that goes back to the time of the Pharoahs.

My deepest thanks go to Jennifer Buxton for all the line drawings, to Doreen Duffin (Australia), Penny Inan and Sally Wuornos (USA), Helga Kauste and Marja Karki (Finland), Mia Lowbeer (Sweden), Vidar Jacobsen (Norway), and Cheryl Myers Edgerton (Canada), for information and pictures of Basenjis in their own countries. To Monty Bowers, Sally Wallis and David Dalton for photographs, and to all those who have given me permission to use and print articles and photographs, especially Krys Marzsalek for her research into Basenji artefacts. Not forgetting, probably the most important person of all – "Bunty" Bowers, who directed the Publishers in my direction in the first instance, thus enabling me to translate a dream into reality.

Chapter One

WHAT IS A BASENJI?

A Basenji – what is a Basenji? It is a small, smooth-coated, spitz-type dog, about the size of a Fox Terrier (16-17 inches high, weighing 22-24 lbs). It is usually red and white in colour, although it can be tricolour, black or brindle, all with white points. It has been likened to a small antelope, being small, agile and dainty. It has also been described as being more feline than canine, possessing many cat-like characteristics, such as using its paws to clean its eyes and face, and patting and pouncing on balls or toys when playing. The Basenji is the only dog that I know that will wipe its muzzle clean after eating – this action usually involves the use of the arms of the best chair in the house!

Its prick ears and curly tail denote that the dog belongs to the spitz type, but the pronounced wrinkles on the forehead, which produce the characteristic puzzled expression when alert, are peculiar to the breed. Unlike other spitz, which are mostly Northern in origin, e.g. the Samoyed or Norwegian Elkhound, the Basenji has a very smooth short coat which is entirely odour-free, even when wet. There are four official colours permitted by the English Kennel Club Breed Standard: red and white; black and white; black, tan and white, with tan 'melon' pips over the eyes and a tan mask; and black, tan and white, without 'melon' pips. The Americans and Canadians now include another colour, brindle. The coat should be fine, smooth and glossy, with clear demarcations between the colours.

If the dog becomes wet and muddy it will lick itself clean and dry, even going so far as to attempt to clean other dogs and humans should they get in the same condition. A bathroom is a wonderful place to a Basenji – there are damp flannels on which to wipe its face, towels to be rolled on, and sometimes there are wet humans to be licked dry... However, your dog will change its mind when a bath is in the offing – personal baths do not rate very highly with a Basenji. When I was living in Northern Rhodesia (Zambia) I owned a Golden Retriever called Bracken, as well as the Basenjis. Now Retrievers, unlike Basenjis, have a great love of water, so Bracken would find the garden spray in order to soak himself. Poor lad, he never did succeed: the Basenjis immediately descended on him in a pack, tongues at the ready, to rid him of any trace of moisture!

Originating from the hot climate of Africa, the Basenji is not at all partial to cold, rain, or

The Basenji colours

Red and white.

Dalton.

Black and white.

water in general. The preferred spot is a chair in a sunny place, preferably located so that the passing world may be observed, or even better, a chair right in front of a log fire – this is a Basenji's idea of bliss. These dogs can always be trusted to find, and lie in the warmest spot in the house, tracking the sun from room to room as it shines through the windows. A Basenji will tolerate snow, even playing in it for a short while, but should the weather be wet, windy and cold, the dog is very loath to venture outside.

When I returned to Scotland from Northern Rhodesia with my Basenjis, Tahzu, who was African-born, managed to limit his calls of nature to once a day during the cold winter months. At noon, after he had been fed, he would go out for two minutes, then return to sleep beside, or on top of the radiator until feed-time the next day. The long, dark months were passed very comfortably in this fashion, but, come the slightly warmer days of spring, Tahzu would be seen

Tricolour.

Pearce.

Brindle (not recognised at present by the English Kennel Club). Damara Bolte.

out and about, making the rounds of the farms in the area to check out any interesting new arrivals that might have appeared during his hibernation!

The Basenji has two particular claims to fame: firstly the females normally only come into season once a year, usually during the winter months. In England nearly all Basenji puppies are born in December or January, although, with domestication a second season in the summer does seem to be becoming more prevalent. Secondly, the animal does not bark in the accepted sense of the word, although it is capable of emitting a short, sharp sound if it is surprised or frightened. The most likely cause of 'barklessness' is the fact that the Basenji larynx has a laryngeal ventricle that is shallower in comparison with that of other domestic dogs. This feature tends to limit the movement of the vocal cords, thus prohibiting the barking sound.

Although barkless, the Basenji is far from mute. It has a full range of all the other canine

The Basenji has prick ears, and pronounced wrinkles on the forehead.

sounds: growls, snarls, whines, and a few sounds that are unique to the breed. There is a melodious yodel (howl), which is used as a greeting or if the dog has a guilty conscience, and a full-blooded howl that indicates the animal is fed up, lonely and hard done by. Most Basenjis are capable of carrying on a conversation with their owners, usually managing to have the last word. In some African tribes they are known as 'talking dogs or 'witches' dogs', and the more dogs that are owned by the medicine man, the stronger his powers and healing skills.

In spite of the lack of bark, the Basenji is a very good watch dog; its acute hearing and scenting powers will alert it to strangers long before more domesticated canines are aware of anything untoward. Like all spitz, they are very independent and obstinate, and they also have an insatiable curiosity. Everything and everybody has to be investigated and assessed – nothing is taken for granted. The Basenji's reflexes are very fast; a quick jump sideways from a stick lying in the path might avert a snake bite, and the dark of the night holds many dangers – that last visit to the garden before bedtime must be taken with great care. Who knows what dangers might be lurking out there in the dark? Vigilance and suspicion must be exercised at all times, how else could they have survived for so long in the bush and jungle?

Another race memory that has survived is the urge to seek out food for immediate consumption; fruit, raw vegetables and even carrots all find favour with a Basenji. They have been known to pick their own peas, beans and fruit direct from the bushes. Young grass and roots are a firm favourite in the spring – root digging can play havoc with a well nurtured lawn, and does not endear the dog to anyone who is garden-proud. Should the opportunity arise, the Basenji is a terrible thief. In its mind, the only safe place for food is in the stomach – nothing is ever buried for future use.

Basenjis are used for hunting in their native land, and they have the in-built instinct to chase and kill, should the prey be small enough, so care has to be taken when exercising or running free, especially if there are sheep in the vicinity. A dog on the hunt is completely blind and deaf to all commands, however obedient it may be in normal circumstances. For some reason, a Basenji has no fear of traffic, and many have been killed by cars over the years.

This hound is not one that will appeal to everyone; its wild, or semi-domesticated ancestry is not very distant, in terms of generations, from the original African imports. The Basenji has a well-earned reputation as a demolition expert, especially when young, and it is a confirmed escapologist. Once it decides that the grass on the other side of the fence is greener and far more exciting than its own backyard, it will spend hours searching for ways to escape – and it will take superhuman ingenuity to thwart his ambition! A Basenji can jump or climb a six-foot fence or wall with ease, and it finds chain-link is a very convenient ladder. Many a squirrel has been surprised to find a Basenji halfway up a tree in hot pursuit.

At one time I owned a bitch that could have taught Houdini a thing or two. On one occasion she escaped from the garden, and obviously having enjoyed her time in the big wide world, she then made it her mission in life to 'go walkabout' at least once a day. If she thought I was watching she would sit in the garden like a little angel, enjoying the sunshine, but as soon as I turned my back she made a beeline for the weakest part of the fence that she had checked out earlier, and she was gone. When she discovered that there was a Great Dane with a litter of puppies that she wanted to play with living next door, I just gave up! Unfortunately, she went over the wall once too often and was killed by a speeding car.

If your desire is for an obedient, servile dog, who will happily spend days alone in a kennel without complaint, a Basenji is definitely not for you. It is a 'people' dog, accustomed for generations to live freely around the huts and fires of the tribesmen; the results can be devastating if it is shut away from human company. However, if you want a playful, teasing, independent, intelligent and inquisitive companion, who can outsmart you more often than not and has a ready answer should you grumble about its conduct, then maybe you and a Basenji are made for each other. There is no middle road with Basenjis, you either love them or loathe them – so be very sure that you are in the first category before contemplating sharing your home with one for the next ten to fifteen years.

Chapter Two

THE BASENJI IN AFRICA

ORIGINS OF THE BREED
The Basenji is a natural breed of great antiquity with a history going further back than written record; its presence has been recorded in Egyptian engravings, both as a family pet and as a hunting dog. Basenji-type dogs have been depicted in various drawings; one by the name of 'Xalmes' is shown in a tomb engraving, dated pre-3000 BC, sitting under his master's chair. Chatsworth House in Derbyshire has a limestone stele depicting Renu and his wife Dedet of the 11th Dynasty (1900 BC) with a Basenji sitting under Renu's chair. At the Saggara Pyramid there is an engraving of prick-eared, curly-tailed dogs taking part in a hunt.

Basenji-type dogs are to be found all over the African continent, owned by tribesmen and highly valued because of their hunting abilities. Sadly, in some tribes, if the hunting instinct was lacking they ended up in the cook pot! Because of the size of Africa – for instance Namibia, a very small portion of the whole, covers an area roughly the size of France and Belgium – the distance between North and South or East and West is measured in thousands of miles. This results in a lack of contact between tribes that are situated hundreds of miles apart, divided by numerous variations in terrain; so the Basenjis that are found in the Sudan vary slightly in type from the those in the Congo or in Liberia. Each area, because of a very restricted gene pool, developed its own sub-species throughout the huge expanse of Africa, in much the same way as the Basenjis on the West Coast of America differ in some degree from those in the East. This territorial difference is very noticeable in the American cayote, with many recorded sub-species.

Armand and Michaela Denis in their book *Leopard in my Lap,* written in 1955, remarked on the variations in type between the Northern and Southern Congo dogs. There were colour variations as well; bush and scrubland tended to favour reds and brindles, whereas in areas with a lot of trees, tricolours and blacks were very much better camouflaged. As Africa became infiltrated by Europeans, bringing with them a variety of canines, a large number of Basenjis reverted to pariah dogs, having mated with other species, but to a large extent the Basenji characteristics remained intact, especially their intelligence and their ability to scavenge food in order to survive. In some areas the 'pure' Basenji died out, but in other regions such as the Sudan, the Congo, Sierra Leone and Liberia they were used extensively as hunting dogs, and

*Renu and Dedet,
11th dynasty
(1900 BC).
Chatsworth
House*

*Detail from
Saggara
pyramid*

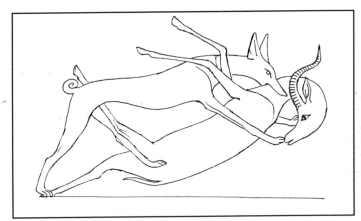

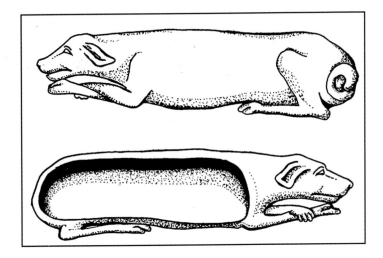

*Both sides of an Egyptian
cosmetic spoon, carved in
ivory. Middle Kingdom
c.2000-1800 BC. Louvre
Museum.*

Krys Marszalek.

An African hunting scene, first published in the National Geographical.

Postcard illustrating a central African village, circa 1920.

Basenji-type dogs, pictured in Timbuctoo.

The Basenji is still highly prized as a hunting dog in Africa.

Damara Bolte.

Basenjis ready for the hunt in the Belgian Congo, circa 1958.

were highly prized by the hunters. It is reported that some tribesmen held these dogs in such high regard that they cost more than a wife.

This is a breed that can run all day at a steady, straight-legged lope; it has a highly developed scenting ability, and can locate game even in high elephant grass by leaping straight up from a standing position, almost appearing to hover in the air whilst taking a quick look all round (hence one of the native names: M'bwa m'kube M'bwa wamwitu – the jumping up and down dog). Even better, the Basenji is odourless, a great advantage for a hunter. The African hunter, more often than not, carries the Basenji around his neck when he is not actually working. Because the Basenji is barkless it is fitted with a bell, made from a dried gourd with a monkey bone-clapper or filled with pebbles, that is fixed around its neck or loin. Generally, the dog is used as a beater, driving the game towards nets manned by hunters, who then dispatch the animals. The Basenji is fast and is quite capable of killing small animals, such as hares, without any assistance. It will also circle an animal at great speed, thus holding it at bay until the hunter arrives to deal with it.

Numerous writers and explorers have described the exploits of these native hunting dogs. In *Leopard in my Lap,* Michaela Denis relates that she and her husband Armand were in the Belgian Congo (now Zaire) photographing members of the Asongo-Meno tribe:

"After three hours we stopped for water and papaya, which was carried by the porters. Here we saw our first Asongo-Menos living unmolested in their original state. The serenity was profound, the peace almost tangible. This was Africa as it must have been centuries ago. The beauty of these people almost took my breath away. Here was primitive innocence, unstained by the squalid inhibitions of a guilt-ridden civilisation. They stood before us, free and straight, with a piece of raffia cloth, hanging down back and front from the waist. They wore their hair long, twisted into braids, and treated with resin and palm oil which keeps lice away. Their bodies which seemed to preserve the formal beauty of black wood carvings, were decorated with ngula.

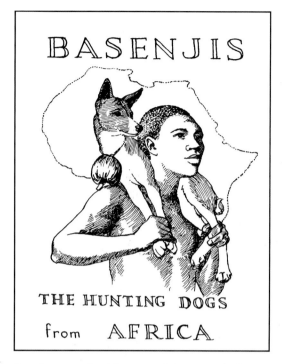

Basenjis are barkless, so they wear a hunting bell made from a dried gourd. Design by J. Buxton RMS.

Asongo-Meno tribesman with a Basenji.

Their general aspect had the hieratic quality one associates with the sculptures of ancient Egypt. The hair-do emphasized the likeness.

"I pointed it out to Armand. 'Yes', he replied. 'There is certainly a connection. Centuries ago there must have been contact between the Egyptians and the remote ancestors of these people. Perhaps they originally drew their artistic inspiration from the Egyptians. It is possible, but who knows?' Their instinctive feeling for art finds expression in bodily decoration, their natural skin colour is copper, which again emphasizes their resemblance, already strongly marked in cast of features and dress, to the ancient Egyptians.

"The Basenji dogs, which the Asengo-Meno use for hunting, were, of course, of tremendous interest to us. It was while I was watching two dogs in play that Armand said to me: 'What do those dogs remind you of?' I thought of the dogs at home. No, not Europe, Africa – Egypt. The strong resemblance they have to dogs portrayed in old Egyptian pictures and carvings. This is surely another link with Egypt.

"The Asongo-Menos hunt with nets and take their Basenji dogs with them; large wooden bells with metal clappers are strung around their necks. The dogs cannot bark, but they emit a strange howling noise and drive the game towards the hunters by the tinkling of the bells. We bought four of the dogs to take with us on our expeditions into the forest, two of the southern type and two of the northern. We took them back to Kenya with us, but the two southern dogs died.

"Loali and Wangu, the northern dogs, survived to interest and delight all dog-lovers who saw them. They were magnificent, pure specimens, uncrossed by any European breeds. Tawny in colour, they have frown marks on their foreheads, small eyes, upstanding ears and curly tails. The dogs from the southern Belgian Congo are of the same colour, though taller and rangier, with tails like greyhounds. I have seen a white Basenji and another type, black with orange eyebrows and a white line down the nose."

Another extract comes from *Old Africa's Last Secrets*, written by Lawrence G. Green in 1961:

"My friend the French doctor was responsible for showing me one of the strange dogs of the world. I had passed it by as a mongrel of the Belgian Congo. 'Regardez le Basenji', insisted the doctor. 'There indeed you have a mystery, a relation of the Eskimo dog in the Congo forest.' I observed a coffee-coloured dog, the size of a terrier, wearing a most amusing look of perplexity. Above the network of wrinkles on the forehead were large foxy ears. The muzzle was sharp, the eyes hazel, the small tail tightly-curled. 'One of the oldest breeds on earth,' said the doctor. 'Old in Africa, but new in Europe. You would have a hard job to discover one in Britain or in France.'

"That was more than thirty years ago, and even now the barkless Basenji is rare outside tropical Africa. I last saw one when I was hunting in Angola just before the war. One of the Kuangari trackers leading me in search of reedbuck, had a beautiful chestnut-and-white Basenji with him, I had not expected to see one so far south. In the deep forests of the Congo and Angola, tribesmen use the Basenji for detecting game, driving small buck into nets or driving them from cover into open country. Basenjis will also tackle the fierce, long-toothed, twenty-pound reed rats which the natives eat. A Basenji will scent its quarry at eighty yards. The Basenji often carries a little wooden bell or rattle when following game in the bush, so that it can be located by the hunters. Basenjis have never become so common in savage Africa as to be worthless, a native hunter in the Congo will give a dozen good spears for a well trained Basenji, some wives cost less than that.

"Basenji means 'wild thing', natives call it M'bwa m'kubwa M'bwa (jumping up and down) from its habit of leaping in order to see over the elephant grass. Of course, the Basenji is not entirely voiceless. No one knows why any tame dogs started barking, for all dogs in the wild state are barkless. They may whine or howl like a jackel or growl like a wolf, but the bark is a sign of contact with mankind and Basenjis have been known to bark... It gives out its typical, plaintive yodel or musical grooo. I find the barkless Basenjis fascinating... on account of the mystery the French doctor mentioned to me 'a relation of the Eskimo dog in the Congo forest,' he said. Was it possible?

"I made enquiries in many quarters and confirmed the statement. Basenjis belong to the Spitz or Pomeranian family. Perhaps you know that the four earliest breeds were probably the pariah, the Spitz, the Greyhound and the Mastiff. One cannot be absolutely confident about the origin of the dog...some authorities say that the people of Stone Age Egypt domesticated a jackal and produced the Spitz, others that all dogs are descended from the northern wolf. African natives will often tell you that their hunting dogs are derived from foxes but there is no supporting evidence. Dogs breed easily with wolves and jackals, but a cross between a dog and a fox has yet to be identified, similarly the hyena is in no way related to the dog.

"Whatever may have occurred many thousand of years ago it does seem that the Spitz inherited certain jackal characteristics, when it whines or yelps the similarity is remarkable and anatomists claim to have discovered many points of resemblance between jackal and Spitz skeletons...It is clear that dogs of the Spitz type were carried by navigators from Egypt during the Stone Age and presented to the barbarians in Europe. My authority is Obermeier, who excavated many caves etc, he found evidence in Europe of an Egyptian jackal type dog which was the prototype of the Spitz and from which the terrier was derived. Other members of the family are the Eskimo husky dog, the Samoyed from Siberia, the Scandinavian elk dog, the little Schipperke of the Dutch barges and the Chow Chow...examine them closely and you will see they all have the unmistakable tightly-curled tail.

"Further evidence of the Egyptian origin of the Spitz and his descendant the Basenji has been found in the tombs. Egyptian artists painted dogs very like the Spitz six thousand years ago. Pictures of Basenjis, wearing jewelled collars and led by dwarfs were found in Tutankhamun's tomb...a Basenji of the fifth dynasty was found embalmed and perfumed and wrapped in fine linen, evidently a dog of the Egyptian royal household.

"It is possible, of course, that the first Basenjis were found far down the Nile and brought to the Pharoahs as gifts. When the Basenji died out in Egypt it survived in the lands of the equator, and is now only really at home in the great equatorial forests, there it is valued as a friend (and eaten as a delicacy) by many natives. African Basenjis have short, smooth silky coats and those with reddish hair shine like burnished copper under the sun. They became acclimatised in Britain and America (like their ancestors in the Arctic) and soon grew winter coats.

"Dogs have changed enormously since the small carnivorous mammal, MIACIS, the ancestor of the whole canine tribe, first appeared forty million years ago. Selective breeding has created such dramatic transformation that a dog may bear little resemblance to its forbears of half a century ago. Yet in spite of the changes in other dogs, the Basenji remains unchanged. It lived for centuries hidden in the Congo forest and flourished when the glories of Egypt faded. And when it was rediscovered within living memory, it was still the dog of the Pharoahs."

In the 1940s Basenjis returned to the Egyptian Royal Palaces when Miss Veronica Tudor-Williams sold four dogs to King Farouk, with the call names 'Mouser', 'Frolic', 'Us' and 'Marigold'. When it was found that the dogs could not travel freight on the aeroplane, individual seats were booked for them – Basenjis certainly returned to their homeland in style! The King abdicated a few years later, retiring to Italy and Monaco, and the dogs were said to have been found good homes.

There is an interesting story attached to these dogs, reported by Clora J. Bradley. When Jim and Ruth Shannon (Jarushan) were in Egypt in 1947, they acquired a female Basenji, called Penny, from friends in Cairo, which had all the signs of being pure-bred, although at that time the Shannons did not know anything about the breed. They decided to buy the bitch a coat for Christmas, and were disappointed when the tailor said he could not have one ready in time. Then he said: "We have just finished a coat for the same colour as yours, for King Farouk's daughter. Since they will not call for theirs until January, you may take it and we will finish yours for King Farouk. Your dog could double for his dog anyway."

THE FIRST BREEDERS
For some reason Basenjis have never become a popular breed in South Africa, and most of the dogs appear to have been imported. There was Antefaa Tui, bred and exported by Delia Williams in the 1940s, and Tex of Alexandria, with no record of parentage but imported from the

Bert Blewett with black/white Basenjis, in 1965.

SA Ch. Taysenji Tahzu: the first black/white Champion in the world.

Sudan and owned by Mrs C. W. Hudson of Durban, who bred under the prefix of Oakover. Mrs Hudson sold two puppies to Monica Marsden of Southern Rhodesia, who was a well-known novelist of that time.

Bert Blewett of Port Elizabeth then founded his 'Of the Jungle' kennels on two dogs bought from Mrs Hudson. Basically these two dogs were inter-bred so much that Tui was great-grandmother, grandmother and mother of the puppies. Around this time, Mrs Whitfield of Port Shepstone owned and bred Basenjis. Bert Blewett continued to breed with very closely related stock, making up at least two South African Champions, Bega of the Jungle and Gorgeous Girl of the Jungle, and then in 1964 he acquired a black and white male, Taysenji Dopa, descended from Liberian-bred native dogs, from myself and Mrs Sadler in Northern Rhodesia.

The black and white Taysenji line was produced by mating a native-born black and white bitch, Miliku, with a tricolour, Zambi of Lindsey, bred in Bulawayo by Mrs Lindsey, a sister of Mrs Anderson of the English Andersley Basenjis. Miliku and a red and white male, Kogi, had been brought down to Rhodesia by Mrs Roslyn Sadler, from Liberia, where she and her husband, Wesley, had been living for some years as missionaries in a village of the Loma tribe, deep in the interior, necessitating several days safari after ferrying the St Paul River. The river provided a natural barrier between the natives of the interior and the more westernised coastal area. It was not until a road bridge was built over the river that many of the natives ever saw or heard a dog that barked, but such animals were of great interest to them. They were taken back to the villages, where they mated with the pure native-born dogs to the detriment of the later. The Loma people were one of the tribes that used the Basenji for food as well as for hunting.

Zambi was the tricolour dog, brother to Call of the Marsh, as featured in the book of that name written by Jill Wyllie. Unfortunately Dopa, the black and white male, had run into a thorn bush as a puppy, injuring one eye, which eventually became blind, thus robbing him of the chance of winning the last Challenge Certificate required for his South African title. A grandson of Dopa, SA Ch. Lazi of the Jungle was mated to Coptokin Copper Bikini, bred by Gwen Stanich and C. Holby in the United States, and the resulting black and white puppies were returned to Mrs Stanich in America. I imported a black and white dog, Tahzu, from Miss Margaret Miller of Monrovia, Liberia.

Miss Miller had a great interest in the breed, keeping a few dogs for companionship and breeding. These dogs were never registered with the South African Kennel Union, but Miss Miller did keep breeding records and many of the offspring went back to the United States with workers employed by the Firestone Company in Monrovia. Tahzu was duly assessed by two qualified judges and registered with the Kennel Union of South Africa, becoming the first black and white Champion in the world when he gained his South African title in 1964.

Other Basenjis that were imported into South Africa include two from Bob Mankey, Cambria kennels. He sent Am. Ch. Cambrias Jikaa and an Am. Ch. Cambria bitch to Mrs Bekker of Johannesburg, who bred one litter under the Andor prefix. Miss Tudor Williams sold a dog and a bitch to Mr and Mrs Paul Jones, Americans who were 'trackers' of the first American space satellite. On their return to the United States they left the dog, Fula Kushkush of the Congo, in South Africa where he later won Best in Show at Goldfields under a well-known English judge, Fred Curnow. Another Grand Challenge winner at the Pretoria Show in 1971 was Pixiewoods Flambee, a descendant of Bert Blewett's dogs, owned by Lance Flight who was only ten years old at the time.

Michael Hughes Halls, in those days a resident of Southern Rhodesia, imported Vee of the Congo, and later accompanied Miss Tudor Williams on her expeditions to the Sudan in 1959 where they acquired the first tiger striped brindle seen in the western world, Binza of the Laughing Brook. After serving time in quarantine in England, Binza returned to Michael in Rhodesia, where he became Rhodesian and South African Champion. A female from the only litter he sired to Carmen of the Congo, M'bunga of Laughing Brook, was sent back to England to Miss Tudor Williams. There the bitch was mated to Ch. Fleet of the Congo and had a litter of four in January 1962, one of which was a tricolour, Black M'Bitsi of the Congo. In May 1963, M'Bitsi and Fulafire of the Congo produced four puppies, all of which were exported. The only dog in the litter, Black M'Binza of the Congo was sent to America, but before going he sired a litter to Confetti of the Congo, which was whelped in December 1963. Four of these puppies also went to the United States.

It has been difficult to obtain any further information on Basenjis in Africa, but I understand that eight were registered with the Kennel Union of South Africa in 1990.

Chapter Three

PICKING A PUPPY

Having read all that you can on the breed, visited dog shows to make contact with owners and breeders, and finally decided that a Basenji is the dog with which you wish to share your life for the next twelve or more years, you are now in a position to acquire your puppy. But be warned – all Basenji puppies should come with a Health Warning: "Acquisition of this puppy may seriously damage your lifestyle!" More than one owner has started with just one puppy in an apartment, but has eventually become the proud owner of a house and garden large enough to accommodate five or six Basenjis.

MALE OR FEMALE?
The choice of whether you buy a male or female puppy is the first decision you will have to make. There are devotees of both sexes; the final choice will have to be made with regard to your own special preference and home circumstances. Next you have to find a breeder. The National Kennel Club should be able to supply a list of Breed Clubs, most of which issue a list of breeders. The club secretary should have a good idea as to who has puppies available at that time, and will be in a position to give advice as to where to apply. Always obtain a puppy from a breed specialist, where it should be possible to see the puppies with their mother and maybe even the father as well. Contact the breeder of your choice in order to make arrangements to visit – to see the mother and puppies and discuss your requirements.

PET OR SHOW DOG?
Do you require a potential show dog? It is important to note the word 'potential'; it is impossible to guarantee that an eight-week-old puppy is going to mature into a Crufts Best in Show winner. All that can be said at this stage is that the pup shows promise, and hopefully, if it is given the correct feeding, training, rearing and tender loving care, it will continue to maintain and improve on the potential shown as a baby. If your preference is for a bitch, do you intend to show her, to breed from her, or will she be spayed? If you opt for a male, will you want him to be castrated? All these factors will affect the final choice of the dog the breeder selects to suit your needs.

All conscientious breeders will put you through a very thorough 'third degree' before deciding

A red/white six-month-old puppy: note the white feet, white chest and white tail-tip.

A tricoloured Basenji: there should be clear demarcation between the black and tan, and the tan 'melon pips' above the eyes is also a breed requirement for this colour.

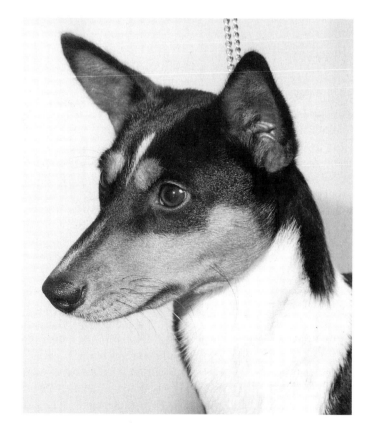

that you are a suitable person to care for one of their treasures. A breeder will ask: "Why have you chosen a Basenji? Do you know all the bad points as well as the good about the breed? Is your garden well-fenced? Is there a suitable safe area for free running in the neighbourhood? Have you owned a dog before? If so, what breed? Do you intend to show or breed? Is there somebody at home all day to care for the dog? Do you have children? Are they well-behaved?"

Many breeders prefer prospective owners to bring their children with them, so that their behaviour towards the dogs may be noted. I did know one breeder of a guarding breed who even went so far as to ask a young couple if they practised birth control! He didn't want his dog to be discarded in favour of a baby that might arrive sometime in the near future.

If you have passed all these hurdles, you will now be ready to pick your puppy. If you just require a pet that will be part of your family for the next decade or so, the choice may safely be left in the hands of the breeder. However, if you require a show dog then there are several things to be taken into consideration when assessing your puppy.

COLOUR

Do you have a strong strong preference regarding the colour of your Basenji? You can choose between red, black, tricolour or brindle (the last is only available in the United States at present). Whatever the choice of colour, the dog *must* have white feet or legs, a white tip to the tail, and a white chest. A white collar, complete or partial, or a white blaze is optional, but the coloured area must exceed the white. A white hindleg or an all-white shoulder, or any other mismark, would definitely count against the dog in the show ring, however good the conformation may be.

REDS are a pure chestnut-red colour without any dark hairs, except occasionally there may be a trace of black on the inside of the tail, usually signifying that the dog carries the tri gene.

TRICOLOURS should be jet blue/black on the body and head, with distinct demarcation between the tan on the muzzle and cheeks, around the legs, on the tail and around the vent. Two tan 'melon pips' above the eyes are a requirement in this colour (known in Africa as 'Gazu Nagi' or 'four eyes'). There should be no mingling of tan hairs in the black at this early age, as this condition usually worsens as the animal matures, with the resulting loss of the required black coat colour. Sometimes a tricolour will have a black bar across the tan on the cheeks; this is thought to be a sign that the dog carries the recessive black gene.

BLACK, TAN AND WHITE or 'Fula' or 'recessive blacks' are similar to the tricolours, but do not have 'melon pips' above the eyes, and the tan markings are often a pale shade instead of the preferred deep tan colour, and the demarcation between the colours is not clear cut. At birth, puppies of this colour can appear to be black but tan hairs later appear behind the ears and tail, and tan becomes intermingled with the black coat causing a 'sabling' effect.

BLACK should be jet black without any hint of brown or tan.

BRINDLE as defined in the American Breed Standard, is "black stripes on a background of chestnut red with a distinct line of demarcation between the stripes."

POINTS TO LOOK FOR

Basenji puppies are adults in miniature; they do not have the floppy babyness of other breeds. As they are smooth-coated it is relatively easy to see the potential in a young puppy, but how that potential develops depends very much on the owner, and on how well the animal is reared and managed during its growing period. A show quality puppy should have good conformation and soundness – a certain "look at me" air; but above all it must have balance, with nothing ungainly

A tricolour showing a black 'bar' across the tan on its cheeks. This is thought to be a sign that the dog carries the recessive black gene.

A three-month-old recessive black ('Fula') black puppy.

A brindle puppy: the American Breed Standard states that this colour should be black stripes on a background of of chestnut red.

J. Jordan Goldblatt.

or awkward about it. There should be no extremes – neither too short, too long, too big or too small.

Watch the general demeanour and movement as the puppies play. Look for the one that is the leader of the pack, moving freely, head held erect on a crested neck, showing a good forward reach with its forelegs. Set this puppy up on a box in show stance and really assess it. The mouth is an important area – has it got a scissor bite? Should the puppy fail in this respect, do not choose that one. A correct mouth, i.e. one that is not overshot nor undershot, but has level teeth with the upper teeth just overlapping the lower ones, is essential in the show ring. Mouths can change when the second teeth appear, but if it is correct originally, that disaster is less likely to happen.

Once you have found a good mover with a correct mouth, then look for other points, such as small, fine-textured, hooded ears on top of the head. A fair amount of wrinkle with side wrinkle is the ideal as, with age, the wrinkle tends to become less prominent. The nose should be black; a slight pinkish tinge at this age may well darken later, but a large pink area is less likely to fill in.

The muzzle should not be snipey or over-long, and there should be no sign of cheekiness in the skull. Eyes should be dark and almond-shaped. Avoid light eyes, especially at this stage, as they will tend to lighten even more with maturity. If they should be large and round, as well as light, they cannot possibly convey the "far-seeing inscrutable look" demanded in the Breed Standard. Those who say that light eyes do not affect the hunting ability of the dog may well be right, but dark is the shade specified in the Standard.

Watch the puppy moving towards you; check that its legs are straight with no looseness in the elbows. When the puppy is going away there should be no sign of cow or bow hocks. All these faults can develop in later life, but if they are present at the baby stage there is really very little chance of future improvement. Feet should be small, neat and oval-shaped.

At six weeks the tail may be up and over, or even have a double curl. The principal detail to check here, at this age, is not whether it is a single or double curl but that it is well set on top of the base of the spine, inclining towards the head. It is no good having a double curled tail that hangs down behind the dog! Basically, look for a well-balanced, elegant little dog, free of any obvious fault, with a healthy shine to its coat and small, neat feet. The dog should be friendly and unafraid – if your choice yodels at you, then you really have picked a winner, whatever its future show prospects may be!

CARING FOR YOUR PUPPY

Before the puppy arrives, check all the garden fencing very carefully to ensure that it is escape-proof. Puppies can squeeze through very small holes and gaps left in wrought-iron gates – if the head can get through, somehow the rest of the body will follow. Cover the pond or swimming pool. Dogs need their own water and feeding bowls. Metal or enamel dishes are best, as most dogs, Basenjis in particular, love to chew plastic. Bean-bags or foam-beds are not recommended. When young puppies are at an age when they are testing out their teeth, cardboard boxes from the local supermarket make excellent beds. These can be replaced frequently and cheaply, as the puppy grows and chews. Worn out clothing or towels make suitable bedding at this stage, but be sure to remove buttons or zips before use. A good commercial product, that can be laundered, is recommended for adult use.

The first few nights in a new home without the comforting presence of siblings may be very fraught for the puppy, the owner and possibly the neighbours. A hot-water bottle, preferably a stone one, or a clock with a loud tick may be of some help – but probably not. I have found the easiest solution is to take the puppy upstairs in its crate, so that it knows it has not been abandoned. Then in a few days, once the pup has become used to its new situation, leave pup and crate downstairs. All puppies should have been wormed at least once by the breeder before leaving for a new home, usually at three weeks, and then again at five weeks. But the dog will need a regular six-monthly dosage for the rest of its life.

A Basenji puppy is ready to go to a new home around seven or eight weeks of age in the UK; this is reckoned to be the optimum age for bonding with people (in America the tendency is to keep them a little longer until about three months old when they have received their inoculations). The breeder should hand over a signed pedigree, the Kennel Club registration certificate, a transfer form and a diet sheet. Many breeders insure the puppies for veterinary fees, loss etc. to cover the first few weeks with their new owners. It is as well for the new owner to consider extending the policy when the initial cover expires.

FEEDING

It is useful if the breeder provides a sample of the food the puppy has been eating in order to avoid too many dietary changes all at once. I have found that a tablespoonful of vegetable oil on the main meal keeps the coat in good condition, preventing dryness and scurf, and an odourless garlic pearl, given daily, is a useful additive providing some immunity against infections such as kennel cough. Most puppies will clear their food bowls immediately. There are Basenjis that are 'picky' eaters but I have never owned one, thank goodness. All my dogs eat as though they have not had a bite past their lips for days! I did once have a dog who had been ill and off his food, and all he would eat for a fortnight were digestive biscuits.

Beware of succumbing to pleading eyes, voice and a skilful love-pat from a paw. A fat Basenji is an unhealthy one, and some can put on weight very rapidly. Puppies are permitted to carry a little bit of extra pudginess, but that puppy-fat should have disappeared by twelve to fifteen months. Do not go to the other extreme, however, and have ribs and pin bones showing. If food should be left after a meal, do not allow the bowl to lie around. Remove it and feed fresh at the next meal.

It is difficult to lay down the precise amount of food required. Most Basenji puppies will eat all and more of what is put before them, and adults have the same urge. One of my dogs once ate a whole pail of food that was intended for six others. It took all of three days before his stomach shrank back to a normal size! Commonsense is the only real guide, remembering to increase the amount of food given as the pup grows. Often the dog begins to regulate its own intake, first by cutting out breakfast – possibly not the most appetising meal by its lights – and then slowly the meals should be cut down to two a day.

At four months give a brunch and supper, plus the bedtime biscuits. At six months give a small biscuit/milk meal in the morning followed in the evening by a supper of meat, vegetables and biscuits. Whether the main meal is fed in the morning, at noon or in the evening is immaterial; choose the time that best suits your schedule.

The choice of commercial food, ranging from all-in-one dried foods or one of the many canned varieties – all of which have been manufactured with the dog's health and welfare in mind – is entirely up to you. Use the food which is most convenient, the type that suits your dog and your pocket. Most Basenjis are fruit and vegetable eaters. Some go mad over runner bean pods, uncooked preferably, some fancy cucumber, carrots, peas or celery, while others have a fancy for

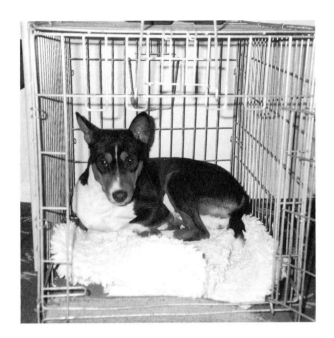

A wire-crate is an invaluable piece of equipment.

fruit – apple cores are usually very popular. One of my bitches would sit and plead for a piece of orange whenever she was pregnant, but only then.

I have read that roots and fruit can form a large part of the Basenji's diet in the wild – a race memory might explain these strange preferences. Certainly they will dig and eat grass roots in the spring. Normally Basenjis drink very little water, but a bowl of clean, fresh water must be readily available at all times. Bones are good for small teeth – they also help to keep a puppy away from other articles that were not intended as teething-rings – but they must be large marrow bones, not small brittle bones such as chicken or chop bones.

HOUSING

One of the most useful items to buy for your Basenji is a wire crate; possibly the puppies were reared in one with their mother, which they regarded as their den. The puppy requires a spot that is its own, where it can retire for much needed rest periods, away from young playmates, knowing that it will be left in peace. A crate will provide this sanctuary. Remember that puppies are babies and need to be treated as such. Snappiness induced by tiredness and teasing at this stage, can easily turn to aggression in later life. Most bad temperaments are caused by poor training, although sometimes diet has been known to have an adverse effect. The puppy will use its crate as its hidey-hole for all the 'treasure' it has accumulated, so the owner will always know where to look for that missing sock! When the puppy has to be left on his own for short periods, it will be safely and happily confined. On car journeys the crate can be placed in the back of the car, and the dog will travel in comfort and safety.

HOUSE TRAINING

If the wire crate is used at night as a bed, it is a great aid in toilet training, as all Basenjis are instinctively clean and loathe to soil their sleeping area. If the pup is enclosed for the night and then let out immediately on waking, there will be no messes or puddles to clear up on the kitchen floor in the morning.

The breeder has probably already accustomed the puppy to using newspapers or a cat litter tray, as needed. It is a good idea to continue this practice for emergencies, but also to take the pup outside immediately after it has eaten or wakened from a sleep. If one command, like "Hurry up" or "Quickly" is used, plus praise when the correct action results, the dog will rapidly learn to perform on order.

When I lived in Africa the doors to the garden were always left wide open. However, when I received two puppies from America who had been paper-trained, they very quickly taught my husband not to throw his newspaper on to the floor when he had finished reading it – the speed at which those two pounced on the paper and performed was unbelievable!

DOG COATS
Originating from the heat of Africa, even after generations of the English climate, Basenjis still hate the cold weather, so make sure that their sleeping area is warm and free from draughts. If possible, they do prefer to be up off the floor and are very partial to sofas, armchairs and beds. There are many types of dog coats on the market, any of which will be appreciated by your puppy in cold weather.

INOCULATIONS
As soon as you obtain your puppy, visit the vet for a routine health check, for advice about future worming, and to find out their inoculation programme for distemper, hardpad, parvo virus, hepatitis and leptospirosis (a rat-carried disease, present in infected water or food). This schedule can vary with the type of vaccine used, but usually the first injection is given at nine weeks, the others following at fortnightly or three-weekly intervals. A puppy should not be allowed outside its own garden until it has had its final inoculation, but because Basenjis require socialising at a young age, they should be given the opportunity to meet visitors, and be carried outside to see and hear traffic and other sounds of civilisation. Do not shut your Basenji away from human contact: puppies need human company and contact.

Yearly booster vaccination shots will be required, and all boarding kennels require proof of current validity of inoculations. By law (UK) a dog must wear a collar, with a name and address tag, if it is in a public place. The Animals Act places the responsibility of any accident or damage caused by your Basenji on you, so check your household insurance policy or take out a specialised dog insurance to cover all eventualities.

TRAINING
After the course of immunization, it is a good idea to join the local dog training or handling club. The pup will become used to mixing and playing with a variety of dogs, and you will be able to discuss and solve some of the problems that may arise with the new member of your family, as well as receiving advice about ring procedure and showing. A certain amount of initial training must be undertaken from an early age. Basenjis are not obedience orientated, but certain basic commands, such as "No", "Sit", and "Down", can be instilled while the puppy is very young. It is amazing how many Basenji puppies think their name is "No!" Never allow a puppy to do anything that appears cute in a youngster, but would not be appreciated in an adult. "No" must always mean exactly that.

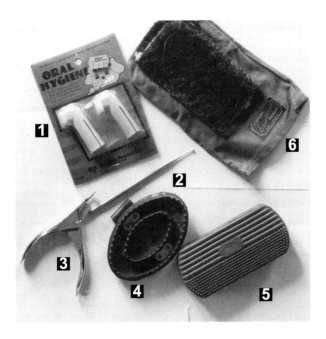

Grooming equipment:
1. Tooth cleaner
2. Tooth scaler
3. Nail-clippers
4. Curry comb
5. Rubber brush
6. Hound glove.

GROOMING

THE COAT
The condition of the dog, and the appearance of its coat, depends first of all on good nutrition. A Basenji with the correct, very fine, eyelash-long coat, rarely requires much attention. A brush down every day, and a rub-over with a chamois leather, will keep it looking trim. These fine-coated dogs do tend to grow a thicker, plush, winter undercoat, which needs to be removed when it dies in the spring. The best tool for this purpose is a rubber curry comb, which can be bought at any saddlery. An extra aid for removal of the very stubborn places around the neck or hindquarters is a hacksaw blade, drawn along the direction of the lie of the coat at a very slight angle. There is a special hair-dressing cream that can be purchased at any druggist, and it is a wonderful aid in removing thick, dead hair. Rub a little cream well into the affected area, leave it for a few hours – overnight if possible – and then brush the coat out. This treatment should remove most of the unwanted hair.

NAILS
Nails need constant attention, they should be trimmed once a week, unless they are worn down naturally by exercise on concrete or tarmacadam. Nails should be cut as short as possible, without going into the quick, which is a painful experience and one the dog will remember, making it unwilling to participate in future nail-cutting sessions. If the quick is cut, bleeding can be controlled by the application of Potassium Permanganate crystals. After trimming the nails,

rough edges should be rounded off with a diamond nail file. If you do not wish to use nail-cutters, a medium-cut rasp is the answer.

TEETH
Teeth require attention, especially the canines. There are proprietary brands of toothpaste on the market that will remove stains, and any signs of tartar can be removed with a tooth scaler. These are available from equipment stalls at shows, or possibly your dentist may be able to provide you with an old one. Large marrow bones, for the dog to gnaw, will also assist in keeping teeth clean.

EARS
Some dogs may get a hard, black edge around their ears. This can be treated by applying baby oil, and then rubbing it off. The condition will probably necessitate a few applications. I have never found that the ear itself requires cleaning, but should the need arise the gentle application of a Q-tip, as far as you can see into the ear, will probably be sufficient. On no account poke into the ear; if necessary, the dog should be taken to the vet for treatment. Some Basenjis delight in grooming and cleaning their companions' ears.

SHOW PREPARATION
When being shown, the dog needs to be presented as clean and neat in appearance as possible. A bath three days ahead of the show will allow enough time for the natural oils to return to the coat. The use of an anti-dandruff shampoo will avoid any 'scurfy' appearance. In America exhibitors tend to trim their dogs more than is the normal practice in the UK. The most that I would suggest is to tidy up a long-haired bushy tail. The American dogs look very neat and trim, with whiskers removed, neck hair scissored and tails and tail-sets improved with a little judicious pruning, but it is an art that requires a lot of practice to make perfect, and if it is done badly it can make a dog look terrible. Providing the dog has been groomed on a regular basis, a final rub-over with a chamois leather before entering the ring to enhance the natural shine on the coat is probably all that is required. Under English Kennel Club Rules, the use of chalk and of most coat preparations is forbidden.

Chapter Four

THE BREED STANDARD

The Breed Standard is the blue print for a breed drawn up by a committee, which if adhered to, should produce the perfect dog for that particular breed. The faultless dog has yet to be produced, but the Standard sets breeders ideal, though theoretically unattainable, goals. It guides judges – especially those not familiar with the breed – and it guides prospective puppy purchasers to find correct and acceptable specimens of the breed. Depending on whether the reader of the Standard is a breeder or a judge, it can be interpreted in more than one way, with some people placing more emphasis on one particular point than others. A breeder will produce dogs that are closest to his interpretation of the Standard, while a judge will place in order of merit those that come nearest his ideal dog of that breed. These are not always the same dogs, but hopefully the final results are not too far apart, although there will always be differences of opinion.

For untold generations the Basenji has been the hunting dog of the Sudanese and Congolese natives. Today, in the Western world, the dog is still the same graceful antelope-like animal, but it has been improved anatomically by careful breeding in order to fit our present-day Standard. The first Basenji Breed Standard was formulated in 1939 by Lady Helen Nutting, Lady Kitty Ritson (later to be associated with Finnish Spitz), Olivia Burns, Mr K. B. Smith, who was familiar with the breed in Central Africa, Veronica Tudor Williams and Major George Richards MC, a District Commissioner from the swamp country of the Southern Sudan with a keen interest in Basenjis, relying on them for companionship and alert guards in his lonely outpost. His favourite dog had been taken by a leopard while defending his home. Major Richards brought two Basenjis back to England with him in the early 1930s; one died of pneumonia on the boat, the other, Nyenabim, died shortly after arrival from a kidney complaint.

This Standard was ratified on the 24th June 1942 by the newly formed Basenji Club of Great Britain. Among the members present were: Miss Tudor Williams, Diana Berry, Mr and Mrs Cardew, Olivia Burns, Lady Helen Nutting, Madie Howis, Mr and Mrs Cutler, and Mrs Kerry. At the Annual General Meeting of the Club on 29th April 1946 the following additions were made:
WEIGHT Approximately 22lbs bitches, 24lbs dogs.

Nyenabim, a 'mahogany' tricolour brought back from the Southern Sudan by Major Richards in the early 1930s.

COLOUR Creams are banned from showing and breeding. (Note: Bongo of Blean sired creams. Bokoto of Blean produced them.)

1942 BRITISH BREED STANDARD

HEIGHT Approximately 16 inches bitches. 17 inches dogs.
HEAD Medium width, not coarse, tapering towards the eyes, well chiselled with lofty carriage. The skull should be flat, the foreface should taper from eye to muzzle and should be shorter than the skull. Teeth should be level. Wrinkles appear on the forehead when ears are pricked, giving a puzzled expression. These are special characteristics of the Basenji but exaggerated wrinkle is to be avoided as the excessive loose skin tends to give a Bloodhoundy appearance and spoils the clean lines of the breed.
NOSE Black greatly desired but a pinkish tinge should not penalise an otherwise first class specimen.
EARS Should be pointed and erect, set well forward and of fine texture.
EYES Dark hazel, almond shaped, small, deep-set and far-seeing.
NECK Of sufficient length, well crested and slightly full at the base of the throat. It should be well set into flat laid back shoulders.
CHEST Deep and of medium width.
BODY The body should be short and level. The ribs well sprung with plenty of heart room and deep brisket, short coupled and ending in a definite waist.
LEGS Straight with clean bone and well defined sinews. Pasterns straight rather than otherwise but not of the Fox Terrier type.

FEET Small, narrow with well arched toes.

HINDQUARTERS Should be strong and muscular with hocks well let down and turned neither in nor out, with long second thighs.

TAIL Should be set on top and curled tightly over to one side.

COLOUR Chestnut with white points and tail tip, also black and white and black tan and white.

COAT Short and silky. Skin very pliant.

MOVEMENT Both hindlegs and forelegs should be carried straight forward with swinging stride, greatly resembling that of a racehorse trotting full out, this swift tireless running gait being a special characteristic of the breed.

GENERAL CHARACTERISTICS Basenjis do not bark. The appearance should be one of springy poise and alertness, greatly resembling an antelope.

This was the Standard accepted by the Basenji Club of America and approved by the American Kennel Club on 9th November 1943. There was one addition made to the English Standard: 'Fawn and white' was included in the 'Colour' paragraph.

A photograph of Kasui of the Congo (born 29th December 1937) illustrates a concise, expressive Standard (not an official one) that is not dated, but which was presumably printed around 1939 as it is the only one to mention rounded cushions on the muzzle and the recommended height as being 16 and 15 inches.

Kasui of the Congo.

Fall.

BASENJI STANDARD OF POINTS

GENERAL APPEARANCE Smart and alert, with poise and stance rather resembling an antelope and gait rather like that of a horse.

HEIGHT at shoulders Dogs 16 inches, bitches 15 inches.

WEIGHT Dogs about 24lbs, bitches 22lbs.
HEAD Wide between the ears with flat skull tapering to the eyes.
MUZZLE Small and foxy, but with rounded cushions.
EARS Pointed, carried stiffly erect, placed well forward and pricked to form definite wrinkles on skull and groove. These wrinkles are an important characteristic of the breed.
EYES Hazel, small and deep set.
NOSE Black desired but pinky nose not a fault.
TEETH Strong and level.
NECK Fairly long, well let into laid-back shoulders.
CHEST Deep, with plenty of heart room.
BACK Short and straight, with definite waist.
TAIL Curled, carried well over haunches on one side or other.
LEGS Straight with good bone and sinew, strong quarters, hocks well let down, rather long second thighs, springy pasterns, feet narrow with high arched toes.
COAT AND SKIN Coat very short and silky, with very pliant skin.
COLOUR Red, black or black and tan, with white points. Light colours permissible but not desired.

In 1965 a new British Breed Standard was formulated; this enlarged on many of the previous descriptions, in particular the teeth were specified as being level with a scissor bite, the upper teeth slightly over-lapping and touching the lower teeth. The colour was stated as pure, bright red, instead of chestnut as previously. Faults were listed for the first time as:
"Coarse, domed or peaked skull. Muzzle too long or too broad. Cheekiness. Mouth over-shot or under-shot. Round or light eyes. Ears set too low or too large. Wide chest, barrel ribs, shelly brisket. Short on the leg. Out at elbows, toeing in. Heavy bone, cow hocks, low set or straight tail, thin open flat feet. Long or heavy coat. Creams, sables or other colours than those defined in the Colour paragraph should be heavily penalised. Poor temperament."

In 1986 the Kennel Club simplified all Breed Standards making them uniform in layout and phrasing. It is interesting to compare this with the American Breed Standard, drawn up in 1991, and I have added my own comments and interpretation after each separate heading. The FCI Standard, used throughout Europe, follows the British version except that Basenjis are placed in the Spitz Group (excluding Holland where they are classified in the Hound Group, as they are in Britain and America). Australia's Standard is the same as the British, although there may be a change in the future now that the Australian Kennel Club is affiliated with the FCI. Canada follows the American Standard, and has accepted brindle as a recognised colour.

THE BRITISH BREED STANDARD (1986)

GENERAL APPEARANCE
Lightly built, finely boned aristocratic-looking animal, high on leg compared with its length. Always poised, alert and intelligent. Wrinkled head, with pricked ears, proudly carried on a well arched neck. Deep brisket runs up into a definite waist, tail tightly curled presenting a picture of a well balanced dog of gazelle-like grace.

Points Of Anatomy

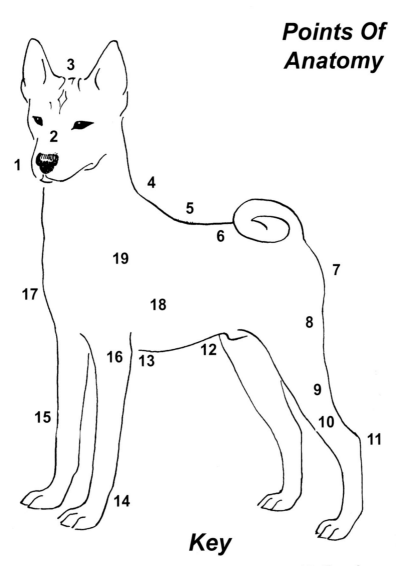

Key

1. Muzzle
2. Stop
3. Occiput
4. Withers
5. Back
6. Loin
7. Reach of Buttock

8. Thigh
9. Second Thigh
10. Stifle
11. Hock Joint
12. Tuck Up
13. Brisket
14. Pastern

15. Foreleg
16. Elbow
17. Point of Chest
18. Ribs
19. Shoulder

Breed Points

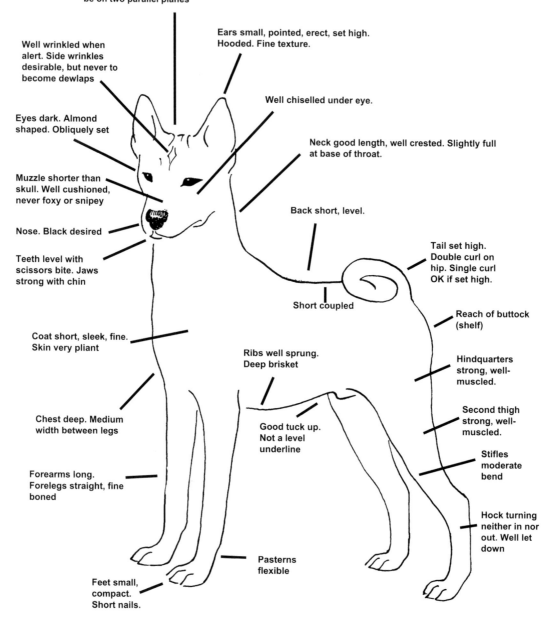

Head carried proudly, skull flat. Moderate distance between ears. Muzzle shorter than skull. Slight stop. Skull and muzzle should be on two parallel planes

Ears small, pointed, erect, set high. Hooded. Fine texture.

Well wrinkled when alert. Side wrinkles desirable, but never to become dewlaps

Well chiselled under eye.

Eyes dark. Almond shaped. Obliquely set

Neck good length, well crested. Slightly full at base of throat.

Muzzle shorter than skull. Well cushioned, never foxy or snipey

Back short, level.

Nose. Black desired

Tail set high. Double curl on hip. Single curl OK if set high.

Teeth level with scissors bite. Jaws strong with chin

Short coupled

Reach of buttock (shelf)

Coat short, sleek, fine. Skin very pliant

Ribs well sprung. Deep brisket

Hindquarters strong, well-muscled.

Second thigh strong, well-muscled.

Chest deep. Medium width between legs

Good tuck up. Not a level underline

Stifles moderate bend

Forearms long. Forelegs straight, fine boned

Hock turning neither in nor out. Well let down

Pasterns flexible

Feet small, compact. Short nails.

CHARACTERISTICS
Barkless but not mute, its own special noise a mixture of a chortle and a yodel. Remarkable for its cleanliness in every way.

TEMPERAMENT
An intelligent, independent but affectionate and alert breed. Can be aloof with strangers.

HEAD AND SKULL
Flat, well chiselled and medium width, tapering towards nose with slight stop. Distance from top of head to stop slightly more than from stop to tip of nose. Side lines of skull taper gradually towards mouth giving a clean cheeked appearance. Fine and profuse wrinkles appearing on forehead when ears pricked but not exaggerated into dewlap. Wrinkles more noticeable in puppies, but because of lack of shadowing, not as noticeable in tricolours: black nose desirable.

EYES Dark, almond shaped, obliquely set, far seeing and rather inscrutable in expression.

EARS Small, pointed, erect and slightly hooded, of fine texture, set well forward on top of the head, tip of ear nearer centre of skull than outside base.

MOUTH Jaws strong with perfect, regular and complete scissor bite i.e. the upper teeth closely overlap the lower teeth and set square to the jaw.

NECK
Strong and of good length, without thickness, well crested and slightly full at the base of the throat with a graceful curve, accentuating crest. Well set into shoulders giving head a 'lofty' carriage.

FOREQUARTERS
Shoulders well laid back, muscular, not loaded. Elbows tucked in against brisket. When viewed from front elbows in line with ribs and legs should continue in a straight line to ground giving a medium front. Forelegs straight with fine bone and very long forearms. Pasterns good length, straight and flexible.

BODY
Balanced with short level back. Ribs well sprung, deep and oval. Loin short coupled, deep brisket running up into a definite waist.

HINDQUARTERS
Strong and muscular, hocks well let down, turned neither in nor out with long second thighs and moderately bent stifles.

FEET
Small, narrow and compact, deep pads, well arched toes and short nails.

TAIL
High set with posterior curve of buttock extending beyond root of tail giving a reachy appearance to hindquarters. Curls tightly over spine and lies closely to thigh with a single or double curl.

GAIT/MOVEMENT
Legs carried straight forward with swift, long, tireless, swinging stride.

COAT
Short, sleek and close, very fine. Skin very pliant.

COLOUR
Pure black and white, red and white, black, tan and white with tan melon pips and mask, black, tan and white. *(In some copies there is a misprint, the word black having been omitted.)* The white should be on feet, chest and tail tip. White legs, blaze and white collar optional.

SIZE
Ideal height: dogs: 43cms (17ins) at the withers; bitches: 40cms (16ins) at the withers. Ideal weight: dogs: 11kg (24lbs); bitches: 9.5kg (21lbs).

FAULTS
Any departure from the foregoing points should be considered a fault and the seriousness with which the fault should be regarded should be in exact proportion to its degree.
Note: Male animals should have two apparently normal testicles fully descended from the scrotum.
Reproduced by kind permission of the English Kennel Club.

THE AMERICAN BREED STANDARD (1990)

GENERAL APPEARANCE
The Basenji is a small, short haired hunting dog from Africa. It is short backed and lightly built, appearing high on the leg compared to its length. The wrinkled head is proudly carried on a well arched neck and the tail is set high and curled. Elegant and graceful, the whole demeanour is one of poise and inquiring alertness. The balanced structure and the smooth musculature enables it to move with ease and agility. The Basenji hunts by both sight and scent.

CHARACTERISTICS
The Basenji should not bark but is not mute, the wrinkled forehead, tightly curled tail and swift effortless gait (resembling a racehorse trotting full out) are typical of the breed.

FAULTS
Any departure from the following points must be considered a fault and the seriousness

with which the fault is regarded is to be in exact proportion to its degree.

SIZE, PROPORTION, SUBSTANCE
Ideal height for dogs is 17 inches and bitches 16 inches. Dogs 17 inches and bitches 16 inches from front of chest to point of buttocks. Approximate weight for dogs 24 pounds and bitches 22 pounds. Lightly built within this height to weight ratio.

HEAD
The head is proudly carried.
EYES Dark hazel to dark brown, almond shaped, obliquely set and far seeing, rims dark.
EARS Small, erect and slightly hooded of fine texture and set well forward on top of the head. The skull is flat, well chiseled and of medium width, tapering towards the eyes. The foreface tapers from eye to muzzle with a perceptible stop. Muzzle shorter than skull, neither coarse nor snipey but with rounded cushions. Wrinkles appear upon the forehead when ears are erect and are fine and profuse. Side wrinkles are desirable but should never be exaggerated into dewlap. Wrinkles are most noticeable in puppies, and because of lack of shadowing, less noticeable in blacks, tricolours and brindles.
NOSE Black greatly desired.
TEETH Evenly aligned with a scissor bite.

NECK, TOPLINE, BODY
Neck of good length, well crested and slightly full at base of throat. Well set into shoulders.
Topline – back level.
Body – Balanced with a short back, short coupled and ending in a definite waist. Ribs moderately sprung, deep to elbows and oval. Slight forechest in front of point of shoulder. Chest of medium width.
Tail – Tail is set high on topline, bends acutely forward and lies well curled over either side.

FOREQUARTERS
Shoulders moderately laid back. Shoulder blade and upper arm of approximately the same length. Elbows tucked firmly against brisket. Legs straight with clean fine bone, long forearm and well defined sinews. Pasterns of good length, strong and flexible.
FEET Small, oval and compact with thick pads and well arched toes. Dew claws are usually removed

HINDQUARTERS
Medium width, strong and muscular, hocks well let down and turned neither in nor out, with long second thighs and moderately bent stifles.

COAT AND COLOR
Coat short and fine. Skin very pliant.
COLOR – Chestnut red, pure black, tricolor (pure black and chestnut red) or brindle (black stripes on a background of chestnut red) all with white feet, chest and tail tip. White legs, blaze and collar are optional. The amount of white should never predominate over primary color. Color and markings should be rich, clear and well defined with a distinct

line of demarcation between the black and reds of tricolors and the stripes on brindles.

GAIT
Swift, tireless trot. Stride is long, smooth, effortless, and the topline remains level. Coming and going the straight column of bones from shoulder-joint to foot, and from hip-joint to pad remains unbroken, converging towards the center line under the body. The faster the trot, the greater the convergence.

TEMPERAMENT
An intelligent, independent but affectionate and alert breed. Can be aloof with strangers.

Reproduced by kind permission of the American Kennel Club.

INTERPRETATION OF THE BREED STANDARD

GENERAL APPEARANCE
It is emphasised that a Basenji gives the appearance of an upright square, the height from the top of the withers to the ground being equal to the distance from the point of the chest to the reach of the buttock. Short legs and/or a long body give a rectangular appearance that is completely wrong.

A Basenji typifying the breed's fine-boned, aristocratic appearance.

Dalton.

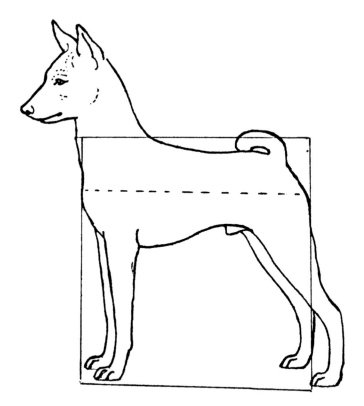

A Basenji should give the appearance of an upright square.

CHARACTERISTICS

The description "resembling a racehorse trotting full out" has caused many discussions in the past. Personally, I think it is descriptive of the Basenji gait as is that other horse term 'daisy cutting' but it no longer features in the British version. The breed as seen in the British show ring today is in danger of losing this typical gait which is so characteristic of the Basenji.

TEMPERAMENT

Bad temperament should always be penalised in the ring. In America any sign of growling or biting results in the dog being dismissed from further competition. That rule should be applied universally. Never approach a Basenji from the rear without warning; its reflexes are very sharp as many a judge has discovered.

HEAD AND SKULL

There should be no sign of 'cheekiness' in the head – possibly this fault is more apparent in males than females. An overhead view of the head should show the smooth transition of the skull into the muzzle with an imperceptible stop. Too much stop produces a 'foxy' expression, while lack of stop produces a Bull Terrier appearance. In profile the planes of the skull and muzzle should be parallel. A domed, peaked or a coarse skull and muzzle is undesirable, as is a muzzle that is overlong or snipey.

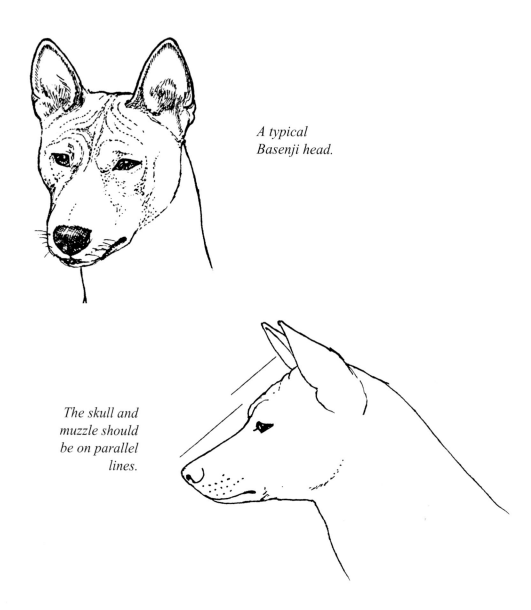

*A typical
Basenji head.*

*The skull and
muzzle should
be on parallel
lines.*

The American Standard mentions "rounded cushions"; this is a very desirable feature, not noted in the British Standard. Basenjis with pointed noses do not have rounded cushions. The bone in the jaw on each side below the nose should have a pad of flesh instead of coming to a point. Wrinkle is a very important Basenji characteristic that is being lost in the breed, especially the old 'Diamond' wrinkle. Unwrinkled foreheads when the ears are erect are not part of the Standard. The expression 'chiselling under the eyes', however it may be spelt, means that the zygomatic arch under the eye should be visible, not 'filled in' by a too broad muzzle and no stop, thus creating the above mentioned Bull Terrier type head.

Narrow muzzle, lack of wrinkle.

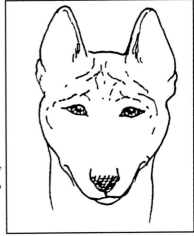

Wide, heavy muzzle, no chiselling.

Light, round eyes.

Low-set ears, wide skull

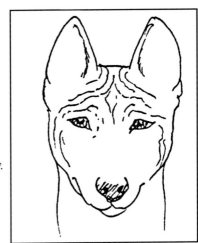

Cheeky.

The mouth: dogs have forty-two teeth; twenty on the top jaw and twenty-two on the lower jaw, which accounts for the two extra molars.

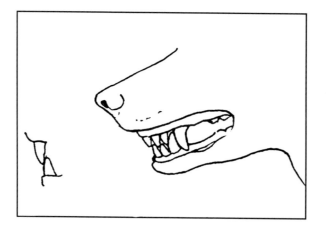

Correct: scissor bite.

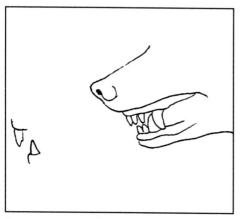

Incorrect: overshot.

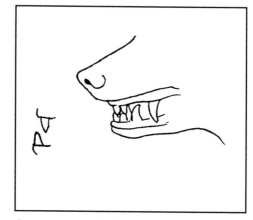

Incorrect: undershot.

Ears should be set high on the head, but require a wide base – the outer side of the base being in line with the outer corner of the eye. This is the position of the ears that produces the wrinkle when alert. Small, erect rabbit ears with no widening at the base will never cause wrinkling. Ears should be 'hooded'. This forward pointing of the ears is a characteristic of the animal and is aligned with a well crested neck. Short, thick necks are incorrect and usually associated with upright shoulders. It has always been a source of puzzlement to me as to why the Basenji – a feral dog to all intents and purposes – which one would expect to have large and excessively mobile ears in order to catch the slightest hint of danger should have 'Small ears' as a requirement in the Standard. Large, thick textured, low set ears should be faulted.

Round, light eyes with a hard, headlamp expression should be penalised when judging. The almond shaped eye, set obliquely with a far seeing expression is rarely found nowadays, but at least the eye can be dark, in spite of the theory that the dog can hunt just as well with a light eye! Light eyes give a completely wrong expression to a Basenji head. Overshot, undershot and wry mouths should be penalised in the ring and it is not advisable to use dogs with these faults in a breeding programme. Basenjis' jaws should be strong with a chin – 'chinless wonders' or 'shark mouths' indicate weakness in the jaw.

NECK

The crested neck should be of a good length and flow smoothly into the shoulders; there should be no sign of what is known in the horse world as a 'ewe neck' and no noticeable angle where the neck joins the withers. A full white collar will accentuate the length of the neck. The head should always be carried high, not poked forward as happens when the neck is too short and the shoulders too upright. The Basenji should convey a picture of flowing curves not acute angles.

FOREQUARTERS

The back is defined as the length of the dog from the withers, i.e the top of the shoulder blades, to the last rib. This must not be too short thus depriving the dog of heart and lung room. Short necked dogs very often have short backs. The loin is the area between the last rib and the front of the pelvic bone, and this is the area that should be short to give the overall impression of a short back. The loin may be slightly longer in females than males to allow room for future puppies. The topline should always be level: not dipped, roached, or high or low at the withers or hindquarters. Ribs should be moderately sprung. Slab-sided ribs do not allow enough space for heart and lungs.

The American Standard mentions an important point that is not included in the British version: "Slight forechest in front of point of shoulder". This requirement ensures that you do not get a terrier front which is completely wrong in a Basenji, as are terrier type upright pasterns. The chest should be of medium width; this will contribute to correct movement as will a good length of upper arm and a lay back of shoulder. Chests that are too wide, too narrow or steeple chested are incorrect and can inhibit correct movement of

Correct forequarters.

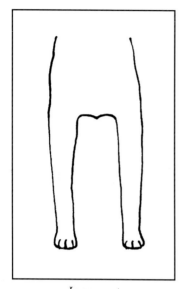

Incorrect:
chest too wide.

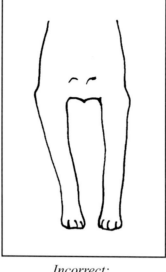

Incorrect:
elbows out, toes in.

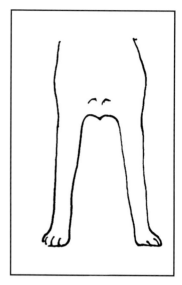

Incorrect:
feet out.

the front legs. The brisket should reach down as far as the line of the elbows, and there should be a definite waist. The 'tuck-up' is another Basenji characteristic; a straight underline is undesirable

HINDQUARTERS

'Moderate angulation' are the important words applied to the hindquarters. Over-angulation will cause all kinds of movement problems – over-reaching and crabbing being just two – whereas a straight stifle as in a Chow will result in a stilted hind movement without drive. Hocks should be 'well let down', that is, the distance measured from the hock to the ground is minimal. Viewed from behind, while standing or moving, the hocks should not bend inwards towards each other (cow hocks) nor outwards (bow or open hocks).

Hocks can be subluxated or double-jointed, that is, if pressure is applied at the point of the hock the whole joint will bend forwards towards the front. This is an inherited condition which can enhance profile movement with what appears to be a good kick-back, but when looked at 'going away', the looseness and lateral movement of the joints can be clearly seen. The opposite type of hock is also present occasionally, that is, 'sickle hocks' when the joint is fixed in one position and is incapable of backward flexion. Second thighs should be a good length. Short second thighs and high hocks are undesirable features.

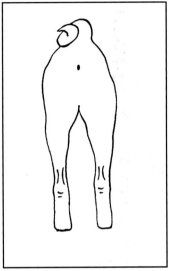

Correct.

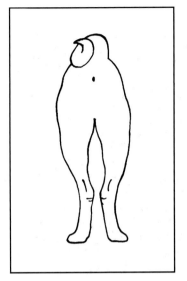

*Incorrect:
cow hocked.*

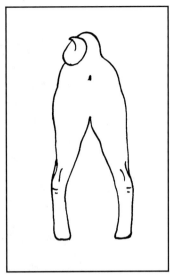

*Incorrect:
open hocked.*

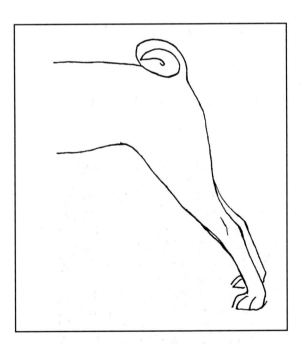

*Straight stifle,
subluxation of
hocks.*

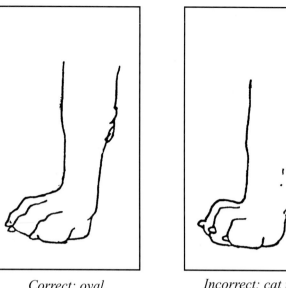

Correct: oval.

Incorrect: cat foot.

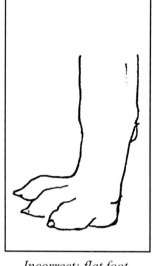

Incorrect: flat foot.

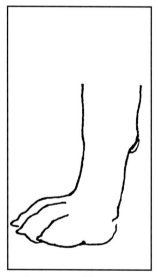

Incorrect: Hare foot.

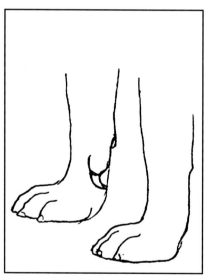

Position of dew claw – these are usually removed.

FEET

Good, compact feed are a "must" for a hunting dog that is required to be capable of running at a steady trot for hours on end. Thin, flat chicken feet or as the Australians call them 'chooks' feet' would not do the job required of them. Cat feet are also incorrect.

TAIL

The most important feature of the tail is not whether or not it has the 'double curl'. So many new judges, whose only knowledge of Basenjis is that they have prick ears and curly tails, straighten the tail in order to see if it will curl again. However, the important factor is for the tail to be 'set on' high at the base of the spine, in relation to the croup, and to curl over the thigh to one side or the other. A tail curled on top of the back or one with a single curl are minor faults, provided the 'set on' is correct, and should not be penalised unduly.

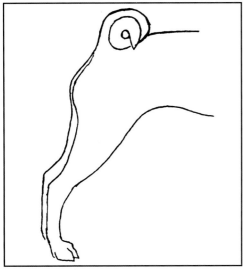

*Correct: High-set tail,
good reach of buttock.*

*Incorrect:
Central 'teapot' curl,*

Incorrect: lacking reach of buttock.

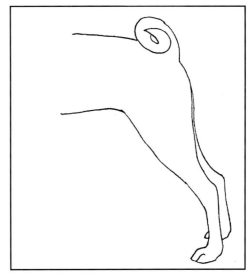

Incorrect: low-set tail.

Movement viewed from the front.

Correct: forelegs straight, elbows close together.

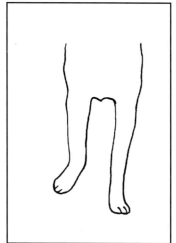

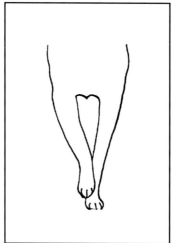

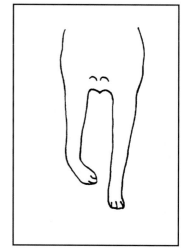

Incorrect: toeing out.   *Incorrect: close in front.*   *Incorrect: toeing in, paddling.*

GAIT/MOVEMENT

To my mind, the American description is far superior to the British version, which gives little or no indication as to the unique Basenji movement. The front legs should be straight, extending as far forward as possible, with no flexion of the pastern joint. Hackney action, while eye-catching, is completely wrong and restricts the amount of ground that should be covered at a stride.

The rear leg should reach well under the body (without over-reaching), while the follow-

Movement viewed from the rear.

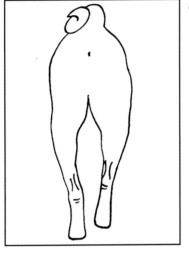

Correct.

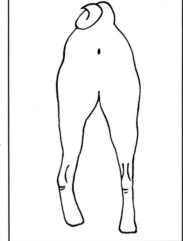

Incorrect:
too wide,
open hocks.

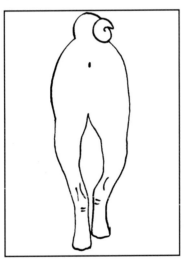

Incorrect:
cow hocked.

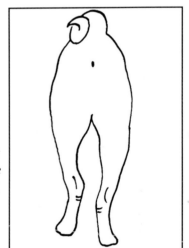

Incorrect:
close
behind.

through of the opposite leg should extend about twice the distance behind, allowing the paw to be seen at full extension. In profile, the Basenji movement is absolutely effortless – a steady, extended trot that can be maintained for hours at a time. Speed is not the criterion here; effortless, flowing movement is the requirement. The topline must be held level. There should be no 'running downhill', a sign of low-set withers and short upper arms. Short upper arms and straight shoulders will cause short, choppy movement and pounding action with the front feet.

S. N. Ch. Sweet Conclusion of Dormtiki's Azenda on the move: note the straight front legs.

COAT AND COLOUR

Skin texture is important; it should be strong but very pliant so that any cuts or nicks incurred whilst hunting in thick bush may be of a minor nature. A thick skin cannot produce the fine wrinkles specified as a breed characteristic. The hair is eyelash short and silk, but with a feeling of bristles if stroked against the lie of the hair. A handful of skin may be picked up without causing the dog any distress. Thick, long hair should be penalised as being untypical, although of course most Basenjis will grow a thicker coat during the winter months in cold countries.

Once again, I think the Americans have the correct phrasing when they specify "the amount of white should never predominate over primary color." Dogs with too much white or mismarks have always been a subject for debate. Some dogs have been of such outstanding virtue that they have won in spite of an all-white hindleg or white shoulders, but, generally speaking, such markings distract from the overall picture of the dog and should have some bearing on the placement in the show ring. Ideally the white should not reach above the hock or elbow, and apart from the optional collar, there should be no white on the body.

Legs that are not evenly marked with white can create an optical illusion when moving, especially if one hock should be white and the other coloured or one foreleg all white, and the other all red. Islands of colour on a white collar are not considered mismarks. Pigmented spots may show up in the white areas of a thin-coated dog; these are not a fault but do not enhance the look of the coat.

I think the word 'chestnut', used to to describe coat colour in the American Standard, is ambiguous. When I visualise chestnuts, I think of a brownish colour, which is not what is required. The bright red/orange coat seen in some of the early dogs would seem to be lost for good. A black mask on red dogs is not a desirable feature. A few black hairs on the inside curl of the tail in red dogs may signify that they carry the tri gene.

There are no specified areas for tan markings on tricolors in the American Standard, but a tricolour coat is glossy black with tan melon pips above the eyes, a tan mask, tan on the underside of the tail, around the vent, on the back of the thighs, and dividing black coat colour from white on the legs and body, though not at the collar. There should be no tan hairs in the body colour to produce a sabling effect. Black and whites should have a glossy blue/black coat without any trace of brown.

SIZE
As with all animals, regular feeding and care cause subsequent generations to grow bigger than their forebears. These days the tendency is for even taller animals, so that those of the correct size are being considered too small. The answer lies in balance – a small, well-balanced bitch or dog should take precedence over a large unbalanced animal.

FAULTS
I have never been able to make a lot of sense of this part of the Standard; it all depends on a personal assessment of any particular fault, and opinions vary widely in such cases. The final paragraph in the British Standard is out of date as the Kennel Club now permits castrated dogs and spayed bitches to be shown in regular competition.

Chapter Five

THE SHOW RING

THE AMERICAN JUDGING SYSTEM

Dog shows are held in most countries, not always under the same rules and regulations but they all have the same aim – to choose the best animal of the breed exhibited and to award a Challenge Certificate and/or Best of Breed. The Championship requirement for an American dog is that it shall win fifteen points, including two majors, i.e. three or more points at two different shows under different judges. Winners Dog (the best of the dog class winners) and Winners Bitch (the best of the bitch class winners) qualify for points that have been previously allocated to clubs holding shows in each American state by the American Kennel Club, according to the number of dogs and bitches actually present in the ring and the number normally exhibited in that state.

For instance, in California two dogs and three bitches beaten by Winners Dog and Winners Bitch respectively, will gain the winner one point. These numbers increase on a sliding scale until twenty-four dogs and thirty-two bitches would rate five points. California is a state with a large Basenji showing population, so the number of beaten dogs required for a major is in excess of that of a state where very few Basenjis are currently being shown.

The dog designated Best of Winners is also credited with the points awarded to Winners Dog or Winners Bitch, whichever shall be the greater. In addition, if Winners Dog or Bitch is awarded Best of Breed, the number in both sexes shall be counted. If awarded Best Opposite Sex Winner, absentees are not counted, the Champions in its own sex are added to its score. All Champions are shown as 'Specials', eligible to compete for Best of Breed, but not for further Championship points. There is no age consideration in the making of an American Champion (in fact, except in Puppy Classes, the judge may not ask the age of the dogs), and most dogs acquire their Championship before their first birthday. The first prize ribbon in the United States is blue, red being second place; yellow is third, and white is fourth.

THE FCI JUDGING SYSTEM

Under FCI rules – which covers all of Europe (with the exception of the UK) – dogs may only be entered in the Junior Class until they are fifteen months old. They may carry forward one

CAC (Domestic) or CACIB (International) that they may have won as juniors, towards their adult title. A total of four CACs, under three different judges, is required for the domestic title; the last CAC must be won a full year after the first was awarded. In Scandinavia, the dog must be two years old before it can become a Champion. The International title follows much the same rules – two CACIBs in the home country, plus two CACIBs in two other countries under three different judges. The last CACIB must be won a full year after the first. Winners of the lower classes are not eligible for Best of Breed or Best of Sex; only Open and Champion class winners may compete for the top awards.

THE BRITISH JUDGING SYSTEM

In the UK dogs must win three Challenge Certificates, under three different judges; the qualifying CC must be won after the dog's first birthday, so in effect, it is possible for a mature puppy to win four or even five CCs but never achieve its Championship should its early potential not materialise as an adult. Challenge Certificates are allocated by the English Kennel Club to Championship Show Societies, the total number available for competition for each breed being calculated every second year from the number of dogs of the breed currently being shown in Championship shows (absentees are not included in the final total). Rules regarding Championship status in Australia and Ireland are detailed in the appropriate Chapters.

QUALIFICATIONS FOR JUDGES

All national Kennel Clubs issue a judge's licence under their own Rules and Regulations. In England, a judge wishing to obtain a licence must first undertake appointments at Open Shows for a period of five to seven years, including an appointment at a Breed Club Show. After this qualifying period, the aspiring judge must wait until an invitation is received from a general Championship Show Committee to officiate at their show. The would-be judge then completes a Kennel Club questionnaire, detailing the number of dogs of the breed that he/she has bred, Stud Book entries and CCs won, the number of shows judged and the number of dogs actually present (absentees are not counted). Following submission of this questionnaire to the Kennel Club Judges Committee, approval for the appointment may or may not be granted. Kennel Club approval has to be sought for every future appointment. FCI rules require an aspiring judge to act as a student judge at at least three shows. After the official judge has made his choice, the student will then place the dogs in the order he assesses them, giving his reasons for his choice. Finally, to obtain his licence, he has to pass a written examination and obtain approval from the Breed Clubs. In America a prospective judge must have ten years experience in breeding and exhibiting; an applicant must have bred and raised four litters of any one breed, and produced two Champions from these litters. The applicant must have stewarding experience and must have judged at AKC-sanctioned Matches, Sweepstakes or Futurities. The applicant who proceeds to the next stage must pass a examination on AKC rules, policies and judging procedures; must pass a written test on the Breed Standard for each of the breeds applied for, and then must be interviewed in order to demonstrate breed knowledge and qualifications.

The Australians serve a period as probationer judges, and are required to pass practical and written examinations on the breed before approval to judge is granted.

TYPES OF SHOWS

EXEMPTION These are confined to Britain, and they are small shows, usually held on a

A puppy should get used to being posed on the table from a very young age.

A puppy dragging behind.

Saturday or a Sunday during the spring and summer months, and any profit is donated to a charity. Entry for the dog is on the field on the day. Classes vary from four pedigree classes: Puppy, Sporting, Working and Open, to the 'Open to All' classes of 'Best Conditioned Dog', 'Dog with the Longest Tail', or even 'The Dog the Judge would most like to Take Home'. These small, friendly shows are the ideal place to start a puppy on a show career. They carry on from the training the dog has received at the local handling and training classes, and give some slight idea of how you and your dog will behave at the next step up the showing ladder. Most exemption shows are judged by a local breeder or personality. No Challenge Certificate winners are eligible for entry.

OPEN/MATCH: The local Canine Society and Breed Clubs will probably hold one or two Open shows or Matches a year. These are advertised in the 'dog Press', giving details of breeds, classes and judges, and the closing date for entries, which is usually three or four weeks prior to the date of the show. Judges will possibly be people who are aspiring to become Championship Show judges of the breed. These shows are, as the name implies, open to all Champions and to complete novices. Classes usually range from Puppy through Novice and Post Graduate to Open. Sometimes the classes are for mixed sexes, or in the case of Breed Club Shows, most classes will be divided by sex. Champions are not eligible for Matches in the US.

CHAMPIONSHIP (AMERICAN ALL BREED SHOWS): These can be All Breed, Group, or Breed shows. They are advertised in the dog press as for Open Shows. Schedules or 'Flyers' are sent to all intending exhibitors. After the closing date for entries, passes, bench numbers and information re time of judging will be sent to exhibitors. Challenge Certificates or points are awarded by a judge who is licensed by the Kennel Club.

BREED CLUB SHOWS/AMERICAN CLUB SPECIALTIES: These are held annually by the club concerned, usually attracting large entries. The judge is normally someone held in high esteem by breeders and exhibitors, very often an overseas judge receives an invitation to officiate. The Basenji Club of America probably holds the largest national Specialty in the world with between 300-400 dogs entered, and judging is spread over three or four days.

SHOW TRAINING
Puppies that are intended for a show career should be given training from an early age. The puppy should be set up in a show pose on a table with a non-slip surface, and become accustomed to being handled by other members of the family and any visitors. It is important that the pup should accept examination of mouth and teeth without fuss. A titbit should be the reward for good behaviour. It might be as well to note here, that it is advisable to hold the puppy in your arms when the vet gives the initial inoculations, or any other painful treatment, so that 'table' and 'pain' do not become associated in the puppy's mind.

When stacking a pup in a show position, use one command, such as "Stay" or "Show", rewarding the puppy for doing as required. Training sessions must never be long or tedious; try to make them interesting so that they appear like fun. Initial home training will, of course, be reinforced by weekly sessions at the local handling (Ringcraft) classes, where you will be given advice on your own handling skills, and how to show your dog to the best advantage. A good handler is never 'kennel blind' and will know the faults a dog may have, and how to show the dog in order to minimise them.

Lead training can also be started at early age. Trial and error will show you the type of collar that suits best, be it leather, nylon, semi-choke chain or a choke chain. Never allow the dog to pull against the lead – that can be the ruination of a good front – and do not let it drag behind. Talking of good fronts, never, ever, pick a puppy up by the front legs. Always lift bodily, with a firm hand under the hindquarters, making sure that the elbows are held against the rib cage. An old mirror, set up in the garden, so that you can view yourself coming and going, will help you to find the optimum speed required to demonstrate good front and rear movement.

Profile movement can be viewed by running the dog up and down in front of the plate-glass windows of local shops on a Sunday afternoon when, hopefully, the streets are deserted. The garden mirror is also ideal for seeing how the dog appears from the judge's point of view when it is set up or stacked. The use of the mirror will improve your handling techniques, and there is no

A Basenji, viewed from the rear, moving fluently.

A show dog must get used to having its mouth examined.

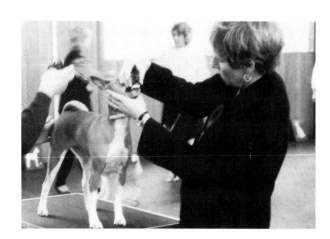

doubt that in the show ring, a well-handled and well-presented dog has an advantage over one that has not been trained.

SHOW PRESENTATION

Care should be taken with the outfit that is worn by the handler in the ring. A dark-coloured dog will not be seen to advantage against dark-coloured trousers or a dark-coloured skirt – always wear a contrasting shade – and beware of long, flapping skirts that will impede the dog's movement and obstruct the judge's view.

Judges also have to choose their clothing with care. Long, flapping raincoats (that rustle every time you move) can be very off-putting, especially for puppies. Big, floppy hats, jangling bracelets and necklaces are not suitable for the show ring. Basenjis, with their acute sense of smell, can exhibit an adverse reaction to strong perfume or the smell emanating from the hands and clothes of heavy smokers.

The Basenji is easy to prepare for a show. A bath a few days beforehand, a good brush and rub over with a chamois leather, and a final trim to ensure that its nails are short, should be sufficient to present a clean, smart dog. Practices such as cutting whiskers and trimming tails have never found much favour in the British show ring, although they can make a smart dog appear even smarter. Pack a dog bag to take with you to the show, containing:

Car park passes and ring numbers.
A cage or benching chain, plus a blanket for the dog to lie on.
A bottle of water, plus food and dog bowls.
A towel.
Titbits (bait).
Coffee and sandwiches for human consumption. (Show catering can be very expensive!)

The ring steward will call the required dogs into the ring, and the judge will probably move all the dogs around in a circle to assess movement, before examining each dog individually. Basenjis are nearly always judged on a table, then moved in a triangle, and straight up and down the ring, in order to check movement and confirm first impressions. The judge will then place the dogs in order of merit; prize cards will be awarded and the next class called into the ring. Always keep one eye on the judge, alert for any instructions, and at the same time concentrate on your dog. It is not possible to keep your exhibit in a show pose and on its toes all the time the other dogs are being judged, but do at least check that your dog is not showing off all its bad points, should the judge glance in your direction.

If you win a class, your exhibit will be recalled to the ring to challenge the other winners for the Challenge Certificate and other top awards. Good luck with your showing: be sporting if you lose, and considerate of those standing below you in the line-up, should your dog win. And always remember, win or lose, you take the best dog home!

Chapter Six

THE ALL ROUND HOUND

There are several activities that cater for Basenjis: lure coursing, racing, obedience, agility, and hunting.

LURE COURSING

In Britain lure chasing comes under the auspices of the British Sighthound and Field Association (BSFA), which holds several meetings a year in different parts of the country. The course is run over 400-600 yards, and all registered sighthounds are eligible to compete. The official BSFA leaflet contains information which gives an insight into the sport:

"Coursing is a sport as old as the first relationship between hound and man. However, in days gone by, it was not always done for amusement but often to get food or eliminate predators. In these gentler times coursing live game is no longer necessary for survival; in many areas such coursing is impractical. But we can still give our hounds the excitement of the hunt through the sport of Lure Chasing. We merely replace the live game with an artificial lure tied to a line and pulled through a course laid out in an open field. These hounds have been bred to chase and they are oblivious to the fact that the lure is only a white plastic bag.

Why Should I Lure Course My Sighthound ?

First your hound will probably love it. Even the most dignified and pampered of sighthounds can rarely resist the the opportunity to chase and catch something – anything! Second it is a great way to keep your hound healthy and fit."

The course is laid out before the event, usually 500 yards or more, including straight runs and some sharp turns. Hounds normally run in pairs with distinguishing coloured jackets – all breeds are muzzled. Hounds may be disqualified for aggression towards other hounds, or interference with another's course, or for causing undue delay in the running of the course.

The classes are:

1. Yearling (1-2 years).

Coursing Basenjis at full stretch.

2. Intermediate (2-4 years).
3. Open (Any age).
4. Veteran (7 years or over).

No hound under a year old, nor a bitch in season, is permitted to run. While the dogs are running they are scored by the judges and spotters, with the time-keeper recording the time taken by each dog to complete the course. The fastest dog is not necessarily the winner. A total of 100 points are available for the performance of each hound, divided into categories:

Agility (25 points). The ease with which a dog can make a turn, balance, keep its feet on sharp turns.
Enthusiasm (15 points). Excitement at the start, obvious keenness to catch and kill the lure, the speed and manner with which the hound will resume the chase after a tumble.
Follow (15 points). The single-minded way in which the hound follows the lure. The ability to search for the lure, should the hound become unsighted. The hound should follow the path of the lure, not cut corners in anticipation.
Endurance (20 points). The hound should not weaken during the course.
Speed (25 points).

The hound with the highest score is proclaimed Best in Field. To date, no Basenji has achieved that honour in Britain, although those that participate in the sport uphold the honour of the breed with many high scores.
The American Sighthound Field Association was founded in 1972 by Lyle Gillette, and many Basenji participants in the sport have won through to the title of Field Champion (F. Ch.). In July

*Basenjis at
the start of a
fun race.*

*A Basenji on
the scent.*

1991 the American Kennel Club inaugurated the AKC Lure Coursing program, with two titles on offer for sighthound breeds. The Junior Courser (JC) title is the first test title earned by a sighthound running by itself over a minimum 600 yard course, with at least four turns. A judge must certify that the hound completed the course in an excellent manner. The hound must obtain two of the certifications from two different judges on two different dates. After a hound has earned the JC title it is eligible to enter the open breed stake in an AKC lure field trial. In this stake the hound can earn the next title (Senior Courser) and compete for the AKC Field Champion title.

The Senior Courser (SC) is earned by receiving two qualifying scores from two different judges on two different dates. The hound must run clean, and work with other hounds of its breed, while coursing the lure. Running clean means the hound must not interfere with or chase the other hounds in the trio or brace. The highest award is the Field Champion (FC) title. This title will be awarded only to those hounds which have shown, in competition with other members of their breed, that they possess the hereditary instincts that enable them to win and stand out in competition. They must obtain 15 Championship points, and included in these 15 points must be two first placements, with three points or more under two different judges. Scoring is on the basis of:

50 points awarded for:
Overall Ability (10 points), Follow (10 points), Speed (10 points), Agility (10 points), Endurance (10 points).
A hound that the judge determines undeserving of a ribbon or placement shall be awarded 25 points or less.
Pre-slip penalty: 1 to 5 points.
Course delay penalty: 1 to 5 points.

RACING
In the UK many Afghan Clubs hold monthly race meetings at Greyhound race tracks, and other sighthounds are invited to participate. Basenjis really enjoy these meetings, emitting ear-piercing hunting cries whenever the hare rattles round the track. Their times are fast too, which is maybe not surprising when I recall a dog of mine that used to run down a live hare over a very short distance. A Basenji possesses speed as well as stamina.

OBEDIENCE
In the UK most Obedience trained and titled dogs come from such breeds as the Border Collie, German Shepherd, Doberman or Rottweiler, although the last three named are being ousted in favour of the Collie. Over the last twenty years or so there have been no Obedience trained Basenjis in the UK that have reached a high standard. Basenjis are more than capable of carrying out all the exercises, but they have a low boredom threshold and quickly tire of repetitive commands and actions. On the whole, the breed is not generally Obedience orientated. However, with a great deal of patience – and a strong sense of humour – on the part of the handler, they are capable of reaching a very a high standard, as the Americans have proved with their many Obedience titled dogs: Companion Dog (CD), Companion Dog Excellent (CDX), Utility Dog (UD), Obedience Trial Champion (OT Ch), Tracking Dog (TD), and Tracking Dog Excellent (TDX). One of the principal differences in the tests held by the two countries is that American

dogs have to negotiate a high jump and a broad jump in their tests. The top Obedience Basenji for 1991 is Avongara Bote CDX, owned and handled by Sally Wuornos (Sonbar). Bote is the first and only 100 per cent African to hold any AKC title, and also the only brindle to do so.

Many amusing stories have been written about Basenjis, and how they have made fools of their handlers in the Obedience ring. In *Dog World,* December 1966, Damara Bolte recalls the story of 'Merlin', owned by Margaret Robertson:

"In the Open exercise 'Drop on recall', Merlin, who had taught himself to turn a perfect frontward somersault, discovered that if, instead of dropping he would turn a somersault, he would get applause and laughter, which he dearly loved. The judge scored him a zero on the exercise, but he didn't care, the audience loved him! At the age of about ten, Merlin could still turn a perfect somersault."

The other story is about how 'Taku', the 'infamous' Obedience Basenji that took nineteen shows to get her CD, and has already been in thirty without a leg on her CDX, received an honorable mention from a judge at one show for her behaviour. One of the stewards was a friend of Taku's, and as she went round the steward on the figure eight exercise she kept trying to get the steward to pay attention to her – the steward kept her eyes straight ahead. Finally, Taku went over and sat right in front of the steward, put her head up and yodelled loud, long and clear, to the complete amazement and delight of the judge, who had never heard a yodel before. Of course, it broke up all at the ringside and the steward finally spoke to her. The judge gave her no score, but he did mention her when he presented the trophies to the others."

AGILITY
These time trials over, under, and through obstacles have now become a very popular canine activity. In the UK, Agility Clubs are an offshoot of Obedience Clubs. Basic obedience is required on an agility course, as the dog runs free and must be immediately responsive to commands. Basenjis enjoy the event and should be capable of doing very well.

HUNTING
The name that immediately springs to mind in connection with the use of Basenjis for hunting is that of Major Al Braun, of the Henty P'Kenya Basenjis in America. Major Braun has trained his dogs for use in the hunting field for many years with great success. Basenjis will hunt by scent and sight. A Basenji is capable of scenting game fifteen to twenty yards away in long grass, and then will leap straight up in the air, shooting a glance to left and right, as it appears to hover at the top of its jump. It will 'point' (by crouching down over its extended front legs and sticking its bottom in the air) and will then flush the game, enabling the hunter to get in a shot. A Basenji will trail and locate wounded game, and can also be taught to retrieve to hand and will even retrieve from water.

The ideal puppy to pick out of a litter as a future hunting prospect is the one that most enjoys chasing and catching a ball (not many Basenji puppies do), who notices birds flying overhead, and who will 'freeze' at the unexpected. This puppy must then be taught basic hand and voice commands at an early age, before being taken on a hunt. In England, Fred Jones of the Joyfred Basenjis trained and used Basenjis in his job for the Forestry Commission. The Americans also hold very successful Basenji Field Trials.

Chapter Seven

THE BASENJI IN BRITAIN

THE FIRST IMPORTS

Basenjis first arrived in England when they were shown at Crufts in 1895, at which time they were known as Congo Terriers, African Bush dogs or Lagos Bush dogs. These dogs were purchased by Mr W. R. Temple, a noted authority on foreign dogs of the day. Unfortunately these Basenjis did not survive very long, succumbing to distemper. At the same time, there were two Basenjis on exhibition in the Jardin d'Acclimatation in Paris. According to Manel D. Woods, author of *Dogs Around the World* , a Mr Stanley Ware brought two Basenjis from the Congo to England in 1917 – a black and white dog and a chestnut and white bitch. The bitch went to a Mrs Glossley, who lived in or near Liverpool, but he didn't know where the dog went, nor if the animals were ever used for breeding.

In the Foreign Dog class at Crufts in 1912 there was a dog described as a Nuem-Nuem or Soudanese Terrier, belonging to Mr G. Blaine. The following year saw the entry of 'Avungara Budwe', a Nyam-Nyam owned by Mr S. J. Burton. These dogs were all Basenjis. Lady Helen Nutting brought six Basenjis into the country in 1923, from the Bahr-el-Ghazai area of the Sudan, close to the Congo border. In an article in *The Tatler and Bystander* of July 4th 1956, Lady Helen wrote:

"I first came across the Basenji when I was living in the Sudan in the early 1920s; they were called there Zande dogs and were not indigenous to the Sudan but had been brought from the interior. As I have always felt strongly that one of the duties of Empire is the conservation and perpetuation of rare flora and fauna, I was most anxious to bring to England, for breeding purposes, several good specimens. A friend of mine, Major L. N. Brown, managed to acquire six Basenjis from the natives, west of Meridi, one of the most inaccessible regions of Central Africa. It took a great deal of diplomacy on his part, for the chiefs who owned them would more readily have sold their daughters and wives than their dogs.

"These six lovely animals were sent to me in Khartoum, where I kept them until I was due to return home. I was by then quite in love with them and made the most careful arrangements for them to accompany me. They survived the long journey in excellent health and created a great

'Bosc', known as a Congo Terrier, owned by the Zoological Garden, Paris in the 1890s.

Reproduced from Le Chenil.

Lady Helen Nutting with two of her imports, 1923.

One of Major Richardson's Basenjis, pictured in the Sudan, 1930s.

stir on arrival in Tilbury. They were placed in quarantine and everything possible was done for their welfare. I was heartbroken when they died of the after-effects of distemper inoculations – which at that time were in the experimental stages."

It did indeed seem that the gods of Africa were displeased, and did not intend that their dogs should flourish on foreign soil. In the early 1930s Mrs Olivia Burn, a Wire Fox Terrier breeder, travelled from Bombay to Mombasa in East Africa, and then across the Dark Continent by whatever means of local transport were available (a distance of some 3,000 miles), to join her husband, Captain Burn, late of the Indian Army. He was employed at the time by Lever Bros as section manager at their palm oil extraction mill at Kwenge. Kwenge was in the Lusanga area of the Belgian Congo, on the Kwenge River from which it took its name. It was the last white-occupied settlement before the border to Portugese West Africa, roughly one hundred miles due east of Leopoldville (now Kinshasa). The map reference is 6.1 degrees S, 18.6 degrees E. A look at the map will show that this was a remarkable journey for anyone to undertake, all the more so for a presumably unaccompanied European gentlewoman.

This intrepid lady used to travel with her husband on his inspection safaris to the fruit-gathering villages in his area. On these safaris they continued to uphold the honour and dignity of the British Empire by dressing for dinner every night! While travelling through the native villages, Mrs Burn became attracted by, and interested in the local hunting dogs used by the tribesmen. In 1936 she succeeded in bringing back to England the dogs that were to become the breed's foundation stock – namely Bongo, Bokoto, Bereke, Bashele, Bungwa and Bassanga, all 'of Blean'.

Less than sixty years ago the journey from the interior of Africa to England was not an easy one. An article published in *The Basenji* in 1972 by C. J. Warrington, another employee of Lever Bros, relates how he helped Mrs Burn on the first part of her journey – the voyage on the *SS Lusanga* down the Kwilo, Kasai and Congo rivers from Leverville to Kinshasa. Every evening the boat was tied up, as sandbars made the river unsafe to navigate during the hours of darkness. This part of the trip took several days.

At Kinshasa, a narrow gauge railway took a further twenty-four hours to complete the journey to Matadi. At this port Mrs Burn and the dogs boarded the boat that would carry them to Antwerp and thence to England – in all, another three to four weeks travelling. No doubt, the Basenjis travelled in kennels lashed to the deck, like those Lady Helen Nutting had transported previously from Khartoum. On their arrival in England, the dogs were inspected in quarantine by Mr Coxton Smith, chairman of the Kennel Club, and by Mr K. B. Wells, who was familiar with African dogs, and Mr Vevers, an expert from the London Zoo. They were declared to be a pure breed and were given the name Basenji – the literal translation of the name being 'bush thing' or 'wild thing'.

THE FOUNDATION STOCK
In her book, *Basenjis, The Barkless Dogs*, published in 1976, Veronica Tudor Williams gives a brief description of the original dogs. The following is a synopsis of her remarks:

BONGO OF BLEAN A male whelped in March 1937. Good points: Ideal size, bright red coat, attractive white markings, sound, well-sprung ribs, compact, level topline, strong quarters and well-set tail. His movement was a joy to watch. Faults: Head could have been finer. A trifle

*Bongo of Blean, whelped
in 1937, imported by
Mrs Burn.*

Fall.

thick-set, especially around the neck. Heavy coat, particularly in winter, feet could have been finer, tail curl could have been better.

BOKOTO OF BLEAN A bitch whelped in July 1935. Similar to 'Bongo', but finer-boned. Perfect conformation, general high quality, movement superb. Faults: Eyes a little too full, not much wrinkle, coat colour a little light – all very minor faults compared with perfect conformation.

BEREKE OF BLEAN A bitch whelped in June 1935. Small, excellent type, dark red coat, dark eyes and black pigment, exceptionally good ears, short, compact body, well-curled tail. Faults: Low-set tail and her head became 'doggy' with age.

BASHELE OF BLEAN A dog whelped in April 1936. More refined than 'Bongo'. Excellent colour, fine coat and skin texture, well chiselled head, fine profuse wrinkle, extremely good neck, shoulder and movement. Faults: Long back, low-set, poorly curled tail, and temperament not too good.

BUNGWA OF BLEAN A dog whelped in March 1937. Sound and showy, a rich red coat, a good dark eye and black pigment, a short back and very stylish. Faults: Big ears with a tendency to 'tip', and a tail with a central curl. He had a tendency to bark, so was removed from stud. Note: Bungwa sired one litter to Kasui of the Congo in June 1939, the offspring of which were bred, especially Kobbi of the Congo. As some of the most noted stock bred in the forties is descended from 'Bungwa', it would appear that his influence had been good.

BASSANGA OF BLEAN A bitch whelped in December 1936. In an article published in 1979, Miss Tudor Williams wrote that "Bassanga's nickname was 'Hedgehog', because she had an untypically heavy coat. She had two puppies, but these were sold on condition they were never bred from."

These six dogs, along with Amatangazig – a bitch that Mr and Mrs Arthur Byron had been given by the Chief of the Zandi tribe, and had taken back to England – plus Wau and Simolo of the Congo, were the foundation stock of the breed in the UK and the western world. Miss Tudor Williams describes Amatangazig in her book as a small, fine-boned bitch with good

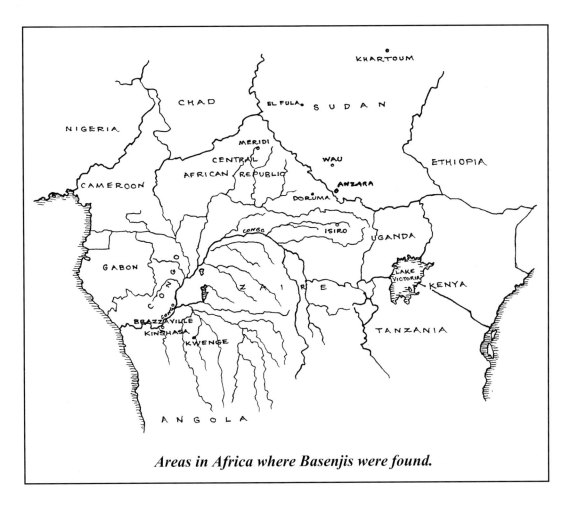

Areas in Africa where Basenjis were found.

conformation and daintiness. Exceptionally red-coated, very short backed, beautiful front and shoulder, and very sound movement. Faults: Round-eyed and lacking in wrinkle, tail insufficiently curled, although well set.

Simolo, and a bitch called Choti, were imported by Miss Tudor Williams from the Uganda/Sudan border, arriving in England in August 1939, just before the outbreak of the Second World War. From photographs taken at the time, Simolo appears to have been a variety of tricolour, with tan 'spectacles' around his eyes, and a black blaze down his nose. He was later given to a pet home as he was felt to be untypical. According to his owner, he had good pigment, a short back, a good front, good hindquarters and movement, but he was far too big; his coat was too heavy, he had large ears, and his head, although well-shaped, could have been finer with more wrinkle, and he had the undesirable central curled tail.

The puppies from his only litter, to Kimpi of the Congo, born December 10th 1940, were coarser and larger than desirable, and so only one, Wunda of the Congo, was registered, in April 1942. Wunda was then mated with Kinga of the Congo in 1941. That line continues down until we find Ch. Andersley Albacore, born in 1951, who is at the back of the pedigree of many

Wait-A-Bit of the Congo, a son of Wau of the Congo.

Fall.

Basenjis exhibited at Crufts in 1937

present-day dogs and kennels. This finding is contrary to the general belief that the Simolo line died out after two or three generations. Simolo's companion, Choti, was found to be untypical as she matured, because she barked, so a good home was found for her. She was never bred from.

In 1952 Wau (or 'Fatty' as he was called, although he did not live up to his nickname) was found near Tembura, on the border of the Sudan and French Congo, by Mr and Mrs McGill, friends of Miss Tudor Williams. This dog was duly registered as Wau of the Congo, in August 1953 – Wau being a town in the Southern Sudan in the area where he was found. Miss Tudor Williams describes Wau as being built like an Arab horse, with wonderful neck, shoulders and long, graceful legs, faultless hindquarters, and particularly good movement. He had proud carriage and the springy walk that we wish to preserve in the breed. He had good wrinkle and tail, and an oblique, dark eye. His coat was fine and of excellent quality. Faults: Nose pinkish-brown, ears rather big, back rather long. Miss Tudor Williams would have liked to see a more 'Basenji-type' head, and she thought that more white could have improved his appearance.

To these nine original dogs in England, two native dogs must be added, found in a shipment of gorillas to the United States. These were Kindu and Kasenyi (plus the almost white 'Congo', who was also a stowaway to the United States.) Bakuma of Blean, later to become known as Phemisters Bois, is also one of the original American Basenjis. So it can be seen that the gene pool for Basenjis worldwide is very small, with just thirteen in total (although Bassanga did not contribute anything). Six Blean dogs (including some of the puppies born to Bongo and Bokoto in quarantine) were exhibited at Crufts in 1937, where they caused great excitement and drew large crowds around their benches.

In the same year, in June, Mrs Burn published a paper in *The American Kennel Gazette*, entitled:

THE BARKLESS DOGS OF THE CONGO

"To go to an entirely new country such as the Belgian Congo for the first time, is exciting to say the least of it. As one slowly churns up the rivers in an ancient paddle-wheel steamer, one expects to see the forests festooned with monkeys, elephants taking their morning baths, hippo snouts protruding from the shallows, and so on; whereas, in actual fact, one seldom sees anything more exciting than an odd crocodile sunning itself on a bank, and sliding into the water with incredible ease and no apparent movement, just out of gunshot. To anyone as canine-minded as I am, the really thrilling thing was the discovery of a very ancient breed of dog, the Basenji, of which I now have a flourishing kennel of fifteen at Bassingham, near Canterbury, in England.

"I have bred and shown Wires for many years but have given them up for this African hunting dog, which is entirely new to England. Seven years ago I went out to the Congo to join my husband, trekking into the interior among natives who had hardly ever seen a white woman. Everywhere in the villages were to be seen these alert little chestnut dogs, the best ones in the plateau amongst the warlike or hunting tribes, such as the Bapendi. These people, as recently as four years ago, cut up a Belgian and distributed bits of him among the villages, thus starting a war and much bloodshed. At the end of the dry season the natives burn whole tracts of bush ... strictly forbidden by the State ... to round up game. The excitement ... and I may add ... the danger is great. Imagine the roar and crackle of mighty flame. Terrified game, antelope, bush pig, wild fowl, not to mention snakes ... rushing out of the advancing inferno ... unclad, gleaming figures of gesticulating natives! Old flintlock guns going off with ear-splitting bangs! Arrows flying and everywhere little red dogs, darting hither and thither, adding more excitement to the scene.

"They will follow up wounded game for miles and hold it down until the hunter catches up. As they run mute, they wear little wooden gourds tied round their loins, filled with pebbles which rattle, so that their masters can follow them through the tall elephant grass. They are of high intelligence and great courage. A female will attack a leopard in defence of her young. The mortality from 'Coy' (cat) is very heavy. It is difficult to induce a Chief to part with a really good Basenji that has proved itself 'N'golo mingi na Kumata M'bisi' (very strong at catching game). They are devoted to their masters, and having a strong homing instinct, if you should make the initial error, as I did, of obtaining an adult bitch unused to white people, it is an uneven chance that you will retain her. After three weeks on a lead and apparent acceptance of European standards, my first was liberated ... and was gone! Two days later she fetched up at the village of her birth, 80 miles away and this, through wildest bush infested by leopard, and in spite of the fact that she had travelled with me part of the way by lorry.

"In many ways, including the extreme cleanliness of their habits, licking themselves all over when wet or muddy, licking each other too, and 'retiring to a spot far away from the house', they are extraordinarily like cats. They are domesticated and very long-suffering with children. In their native haunts they curl up and sleep with their backs against their owners to guard the latter from harm. They have a great sense of humour and a playful temperament that makes them ideal companions. They appear to stand most climates admirably, evolving like many wild animals, a special winter coat to combat the English cold. This disappears in May, when their pliant skin becomes smoother, softer and redder than ever. It is curious that they never seem to smell of 'dog' even when wet.

"A small percentage are black, while others are cream or pale-sand coloured. The natives treasure these light-coloured dogs, saying they resemble the white man ... 'pilamushi mandelli', but the majority of dogs are chestnut with white points. These, to my mind, are by far the most attractive. They have prick ears, wrinkled foreheads and tightly curled tails, to one or other side of the quarters. Basenjis are alert and antelope-like in form, stance and elegance. They are very fast, which is curious considering the tail. For long treks they will take to a straight-legged run which they can keep up for miles.

"These dogs are indigenous to vast areas of Central Africa, mainly in the interior. Some, from the Nyam Nyam and Manboutu tribes are thicker and shorter in the leg, but these were used by the hungry as a table delicacy. Such comestible dogs are described in the account of a journey in the Upper Nile by Schweinfurth in 1886. They are also mentioned by Schebaste in his book *My Pygmy Hosts*, where a photograph of a poor specimen appears. There is a replica of a Basenji in the Giza Museum, Cairo, another from the 12th Egyptian Dynasty, and a dog very similar is to be seen chasing an antelope, on a disk recently excavated from the tomb at Sakkhara, under the auspices of the well known American archeologist, Walter B. Emery.

"In spite of being the father of twelve, he (Bongo of Blean) is not above behaving in the most absurd fashion, and flying, with tail as straight as it is possible for a Basenji to achieve, like a mad thing, hotly pursued by his panting, yelping young in a form of 'Chase me, Charlie'. They 'jink' with surprising rapidity, almost always ending up in a complete 'head-over-heels'. At Crufts Bongo's attitude towards the crowds was laughable. Being tied up rather short, so that people could not touch him, he had not much room to move. So he sat on his rump, with his hind feet sticking out in front, looking absurdly like a brown bear at the zoo, with a look of polite disdain on his face. He trotted into the show ring as though he was accustomed to going to a show every week and took second prize almost as a matter of course.

"Mr Simpson the judge said of him: 'Bongo of Blean, smart Basenji, capital legs and feet, very nice body, tightly curled tail, perfect hindquarters, one who looks as though he can do a hard job.' I was delighted that the judge confirmed my own opinion which is that Bongo is a typical

Basenji and almost perfect of his kind. (Note: Bongo had been entered in the 'Any Other Variety' class. The winner was a Lhasa Apso. In 1938 there were breed classes for the first time and Bongo was Best of Breed.) All six dogs behaved beautifully towards the jostling crowds, which pushed and shoved in their efforts to see 'the little dogs that don't bark', so that one felt like shouting out: 'Stand back and give the dogs some air.'

"The questions were legion and all very much alike: 'Don't they really bark?' 'What, do you mean they can't bark?' 'Can you tell me are these the little dogs that don't bark?' And so on, ad infinitum. By evening, when the crowds were spectators and those really interested had gone, and our heads were reeling and some of our neighbours had gone to sleep on their benches along with their dogs, our own vocal chords began to give out. Some people even suggested that the dogs had been operated on to make them dumb! It is perfectly true that the Basenji never barks. But it does not meant that they are dumb or bad guards. Some asked 'What good would a barkless dog be as a guard?' Well, if I were a burglar, I would sooner face Fido's senseless yapping any day or night than Bongo's unsoothing rumble and warning eye.

"For ten days prior to Crufts we had been infested with reporters and photographers. It was worth it though, because the dogs got amazing publicity and some excellent photographs were taken. We were even met at Victoria Station, London, just like Royalty, by the press. So it was not surprising that inquiries and orders came pouring in directly after the show, to combat which, more stock is being sent from the Congo. At this writing, the six latest puppies are now fourteen weeks old – four daughters and two sons of Bereke and Bongo. They are uniform and perfect: healthy, full of pep and extraordinarily typical of the breed. When I remember the many vicissitudes and our nightmare journey home from the Congo, on account of the serious illness of my daughter who was with me, and my own ill health and the dogs to cope with unaided all the way ... and how we staggered ashore in the Old Country on Christmas Eve 1936, exhausted but triumphant, it seems too good to be true that Basenjis have been successfully introduced into England.

"But this success is not surprising for they are such splendid all-round dogs. They are not gun-shy and will face the thickest covert where a foxhound will not venture. They make ideal companions being no larger than a Fox Terrier and clean-skinned. And best of all, Basenjis make ideal dogs for flat dwellers, for in a world continually made hideous by noise, these little fellows from the Congo do not bark."

THE EARLY BREEDERS

One of the dogs brought over from the Congo, as a result of the interest created at Crufts, was Bakuma of Blean, who was sent straight from quarantine to Mr and Mrs Byron Rogers in America, along with two English-bred Blean bitches, Basashi and Rougi, travelling on the *SS Berengaria*. The bitches and a litter all died, probably from distemper. Bakuma went missing, but was later discovered by Al Phemister and re-registered as Phemsters Bois.

The very first Basenjis registered by the Kennel Club were placed in the 'Any Other Breed or Variety' Group in February 1937. These were the Blean dogs and a native-born bitch, 'Musti', owned by Mr D. Cross, and bred by Mr Capita. Basenjis were entered into the Breed Register in 1941 (28 Basenjis registered at this time) and placed in the Hound Group.

Miss Tudor Williams founded her 'of the Congo' kennels on Kasui and Kwango of the Congo, a dog and a bitch born on December 20th 1937, from Bwacha and Bokoto of Blean. She also

Royal Emperor, owned by Mrs Grazella Bowden Smith. 'Our Dogs' Presentation Plate, Christmas 1938.

Kwango and Kasui of the Congo: the foundation dogs of Miss Veronica Tudor Williams' kennel.

Fall.

bought a native-born female – brought from the Zandi country of Africa by Mr and Mrs Arthur Byron – this was Amatangazig, who was to prove such an asset to the breed. Amantangazig had a tricolour sibling which Mrs Byron would have liked, but the chief wished to keep that puppy. Mrs Byron subsequently wrote a book, *Figures of Eight*, under the name Patricia Cockburn, published by Chatto and Windus of the Hogarth Press, describing Amantangazig and her antics in England. The Basenji even appeared on the *In Town Tonight* television programme, but would not yodel to order!

The war years 1939-1945 were difficult for dog owners and breeders, but the breed was nurtured by such dedicated breeders as Mrs Burn (Blean) Mrs Harbottle-Smith (Bardseal), Mrs Lister-Empson (Ousefleet), Commander & Miss Bishop (Pilon), Mr Kent (Silvercaul) and Miss Tudor Williams (of the Congo), and it was thanks to the dedication of all these early breeders that a viable nucleus of puppies was available once peace was declared. These puppies included Brown Trout of the Congo and his sister Fern – who became the first Basenji Champions – and whose accidental mating in 1947 produced the first tricolours to be born in Britain, proving that Amatangazig (grandmother) carried the tricolour gene. From the resulting litter, Black Idol of the Congo was sent to the United States, and Black Magic of the Congo eventually became the first tricolour Champion in England.

The Basenji Club of Great Britain – the first Basenji Club in the world – was formed in 1939, with Lady Helen Nutting as president and her sister, Lady Kitty Ritson, as vice president. (Lady Kitty was an all round judge of the time with an interest in Foreign Dogs.) At the the club's first Championship Show, held on July 27th 1946 with Tom Scott as the judge, the dog CC was won by Miss D. Berry's future Champion, Sunspot of the Congo, and the bitch CC was awarded to his half-sister – Miss M. A. Kerry's Pilon Dulcinee. In 1953 Mr L. R. Percival founded the Basenji Owners and Breeders Association, and in the 1970s the Northern Basenji Society was formed.

These early breeders had many difficulties to overcome. In a letter dated 1958, Miss Tudor Williams wrote: "The early struggles were appalling, the native stock carried cream (semi-albino), incredibly bad scrotal and inquinal hernias, cleft palates etc. The only way was to take a bold line and in-breed, these faults were everywhere and the strange thing is – it worked!" Listening to stories from past owners and breeders, it appears that temperament was a great problem, as well.

The year 1945 saw the birth of Mrs Anderson's first litter under the prefix Andersley, a prefix which was to play such an important role in the history of the breed. The greatest of the many Champions she bred was Eng. Am. Ch. Andersley Atlantic, born 1954, the first dog to win a record twenty-five CCs in England and then cross the Atlantic to gain his American title, aged ten and a half! Miss Diana Berry's Sin kennels were also founded at this time. She bred and exported to the United States the 'Blue' Basenjis, May Morning and Morning Mist of Sin, in 1963. This colour was a dilution of the tri factor, and did not meet with universal approval. Cream was another colour to crop up in early breeding, but as these dogs were said to be semi-albino with pink noses, eye rims and yellowish eyes, the colour was deemed unacceptable.

Miss Grazellia Bowden Smith of Guernsey, an avid collector of what were, at that time, rare breeds, advertised Royal Emperor, a cream, in the *Dog World Annual* of 1938, and two Basenjiss – Amadeus and Prince Charming – were depicted in 1945. The latter two were from a litter by Kwango of the Congo out of Kookoo of the Congo. From the photograph these do appear to have dark eyes and black noses. Barbara Percival's Littlebreach Basenjis came on to the scene

*Ch. Andersley
Peacehill Pacific.*

*Ch. Jamie of
Littlebreach,
pictured in 1954.*

Fall.

*Ch. Letitia of
Littlebreach,
pictured in 1961.*

Fall.

Ch. Lograk Lubilash of Littlebreach, bred by Mr W. Taylor, the only Basenji to win the Hound Group at Crufts.

Fall.

Ch. Andersley Americana: Reserve Group winner at Chester and Blackpool.

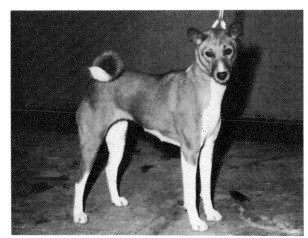

Ch. Siren of Horsley: winner of the Hound Group at Peterborough Championship Show, 1966.

Eng. Ir. Ch. Horsleys Sir Kincaid: current breed record holder with forty CCs and Best in Show at the Scottish Kennel Club Show, 1980.

Zizunga Gilded Lily: Reserve Group winner, South Wales Championship Show, 1991.

at this time, and they included such well-known dogs as: Eng. Am. Ch. Amelia, Eng. Ir. Ch. Syngefield Leonato, Ch. Benedick, Ch. Jamy, Ch. Rolf, and others, numbering twelve in total. Mrs Percival first registered a Basenji litter in 1950.

THE BIG WINNERS

Ch. Lograk Lubilash of Littlebreach, bred by Mr W. Taylor, is still the only dog to have topped the Hound Group at Crufts, which he did in 1963. Ch. Syngefield Leonato of Littlebreach won the Hound Group at Chester in 1955 and Reserve Best in Show at Blackpool in the same year – that show was not judged on the Group system.

Other Basenjis have achieved the honour of being winners of the Hound Group at Championship Shows, but compared to similar wins in America and Australia, they are a mere handful. Ch. Siren of Horsley, a tricolour, is the only Basenji of that colour to win a Group at a general Championship Show, which she did at Peterborough in 1966. Mrs Wilson Stringer was

Ch. Taysenji Yoko: the first black/white Champion in the Western world.

Ch. Horsleys Sircillatar: the first black/white bitch Champion in the world.

also successful in the previous year when Ch. Sir Casper of Horsley was top hound. Lograk Lalhminga, bred by Mr and Mrs Kargol and owned by Mrs Pennington of Breezecrest kennels, topped the Group at Chester in 1958, aged six and a half months. The judge was Joe Braddon.

In 1956 Mr and Mrs Anderson brought Ch. Andersley Atlantic and his Champion sister, Americana, down from Scotland to exhibit in England. It was a trip that was to prove well worthwhile, as Atlantic won Reserve Best in Show at Windsor Championship Show, and Americana was Reserve in the Group at Chester and went on to repeat that win at Blackpool under the well-known American judge, Percy Roberts. Ch. Colonel Phaeton of Courtlands, owned by Connie Graham, won two Groups in the seventies at WELKS and the Scottish Kennel Club.

SA Ch. Taysenji Tahzu, imported by Elspet Ford.

Ch. St Erme Fula Falcon of the Congo was successful at Leicester in 1967. And, of course, Eng. Ir. Ch. Horsleys Sir Kincaid, the current breed record holder with forty Challenge Certificates, won Best in Show at the Scottish Kennel Club show in 1980. The only previous Best in Show winner was Ch. Leda of Syngefield, who took the honour at an Irish Championship Show in the early fifties. Reserves in Group (or number 2, as Group winners are not placed down the line in Britain) were won by Ch.The Jester of Courtlands, owned by Connie Graham, at Dublin and Leeds Championship Shows in the seventies. John and Winnie Castellani's home-bred Ch. Djoser Sekhmet was successful in being placed Reserve in the Hound Group at the Scottish Kennel Club Show in August 1987. The most recent success was notched up by Irene Terry's Zizunga Gilded Lily, at South Wales Championship Show in 1991.

THE TAYSENJI BASENJIS

I returned to Britain from Zambia in 1965, bringing with me SA Ch. Taysenji Tahzu, Coptokin Copper Beautique who was in whelp to Tahzu's son, Taysenji Tigee (a black/white), and SA Ch. Taysenji Titema. Unfortunately Beauty and Titema had a longstanding dislike of each other, so Titema was later placed in a pet home. Copper Beautique whelped while in quarantine, on April 25th 1965. There were five in the litter, and two bitches and one dog, all black, were sent to Mrs Stanich in the United States.

On hearing about the litter, Colette Campbell, of Gooses Basenjis, sent her kennelmaid, Christine Rutherford (now Rix) up to Scotland to purchase the red bitch puppy, Taysenji Tuyey.

*Ch. Azenda
Tuffanuff, bred by
Margaret Christie
Davies, winner of
seven CCs.*

*Ch. Asaris Ti Karu,
imported by Elspet
Ford from America,
won her title at
Crufts, 1982.*

*Ch. Zizunga Satin
Doll: winner of
twenty-one CCs.*

Dalton.

Ch. St Erme Jolly Swagman: winner of thirty CCs.

Hartley.

Handled by Christine, she went on to win a Challenge Certificate and two reserve CCs. The last puppy, Taysenji Samogi, a beautiful orange/red-coated dog with wonderful movement, won two reserve CCs with only limited showing, as the distance to most English shows from Aberdeen (before the days of motorways) was long and arduous, and usually meant spending two nights sleeping in the car and feeding from fish and chip shops. In fact, Samogi became very partial to chips! Unfortunately he took to chasing sheep, so he had to be found a home in a town, thus putting an end to his show career.

At this time there was a very strong anti-Liberian, anti-black/white lobby led mainly by Miss Tudor Williams and Phyllis Cook, who did not consider the breeding or colour of these dogs to be pure Basenji. They attempted to have Tahzu's registration rescinded by the Kennel Club, but they were unsuccessful. On December 10th 1965 S.A. Ch. Taysenji Tahzu and Buckhatch Ballerina, a tricolour, produced a litter of seven, of which the last arrival – the only black/white – was Taysenji Yoko, who in 1969, in the ownership of Mirrie St Erme Cardew, won his qualifying Certificate to become the first black/white Champion in the Western world. In many ways it is unfortunate that Tahzu's new blood and genes were not utilised as much as they might have been in the UK – he could have contributed a great deal to the breed.

NEW IMPORTS
In the same year Jayne Wilson Stringer imported from the United States two black/white puppies bred by Shirley Chambers of Khajah kennels. Sheen and Satin of Horsley were born April 14th 1965; their parents were Khajah's Black Fula Challenge (a recessive tricolour) and Black Diamond of Cryon (black/white), the daughter of Gunn's Rameses and a Liberian-bred black/white bitch, Kiki of Cryon. Sheen of Horsley, mated to Bunty Tress's Ch. Ridingsgold

Ch. Domewood Devil Dancer became top bitch with fifteen CCs.

Ch. Neyeliz Castanea took the bitch record with twenty-four CCs, in 1985.

Fantasia, produced Sir Buntar of Horsley, the sire of the first black/white bitch Champion in the world, Horsleys Sircillatar. There have been three other imports within recent years, but none added anything new to the gene pool as they were all descended from the original dogs.

Am. Ch. Touch o'Class of Woz came from Cecelia Wozniak in America. 'Caddi' spent a year in British quarantine, before proceeding to his new owners, Audrey DeLittle and Jan Roberts of Tamsala Kennels in Australia, where he quickly became an Australian Champion. During his six months residential quarantine in England he sired three litters, and I handled him to win two Challenge Certificates. Unfortunately, he had to continue his onward journey to Australia before competing for the all-important third certificate. His best-known offspring in the UK is probably Ch. Azenda Tuffanuff, bred by Margaret Christie Davies, the winner of seven CCs.

In 1980 I imported Asaris Ti Karu from America. Karu obtained her Championship at Crufts 1982, handled by her breeder Russell Hendren, under judge Ben Reynolds Frost. This was the first, and so far, the only American bred and handled Basenji to win a Best of Breed at Crufts, and her companion Ch. Taysenji Kush won the Dog CC to complete a unique 'double'. Miss Tudor Williams imported Australian Ch. Afrika Royal Challenge of the Congo from Marie Dymock in 1980. 'Aussie' soon became an English Champion, winning seven CCs. He was Top Stud Dog in the Breed in 1985, 1987 and 1988, producing Mesdames St Erme Cardew and Buckingham's Ch. St Erme Jolly Swagman (who won thirty CCs), and Irene Terry's Ch. Zizunga Satin Doll (a bitch with a total of twenty-one CCs).

In 1991 Mrs Wilson Stringer imported Aust. Ch. Pukkanut Night Music from Mrs Hunt, and three puppies which were born in quarantine. These are descendants of one of her original importations to Australia, Horsleys Sir Frasertar. Jane Gostynska has bought back two Swedish-born dogs from English breeding, namely Wamba's N'Shinook and Wamba's N'Caramba.

RECORD HOLDERS

Unlike an American Champion, a title-holder in the UK can continue to amass Challenge Certificates after the obligatory three required for the title. Over the years there have been a few multiple CC winners. The first male recordholder was Eng. Am. Ch. Andersley Atlantic with twenty-five 'tickets'. He was followed by Ch. St Erme Fula Falcon of the Congo with twenty-nine CCs, but that number was surpassed by the present holder of the honour, Eng. Ir. Ch. Horsleys Sir Kincaid with forty CCs to his credit. The first bitch recordholder was Ch. Carnival of the Congo with thirteen CCs in 1955. It was not until twenty-seven years later that Bunty Bower's Ch. Domewood Devil Dancer became top bitch with fifteen CCs. That record stood until Ken Richardson's Ch. Neyeliz Castanea overtook Devil Dancer in 1985, and she still holds the record with twenty-four tickets.

THE SEARCH FOR NEW STOCK

In 1959 Miss Tudor Williams, accompanied by Michael Hughes Halls of Laughing Brook kennels in Southern Rhodesia (Zimbabwe) and Col. John Rybot, Hillbutt Basenjis, went to the Southern Sudan in the search of new stock. In the area around Anzara in the Sudan they acquired a little red/white bitch, later to be named Fula of the Congo, and a brindle (tiger-striped) dog which Michael Hughes Halls took back to Rhodesia with him. As brindle was not a recognized colour in the Breed Standard, the dog was unacceptable to many English breeders and canine politics forced his return to Africa. 'Tiger' later became S.A. Rhod. Ch. Binza of Laughing Brook, in spite of his colour. Fula was bred twice by Miss Tudor Williams, first to Consolation

Ch. Neyeliz Cascade:
Top Stud Dog, 1991.

Ch. Ijnesab Bedazzle at
Jethard: top winning
bitch, 1991.

Dalton.

Ch. McEnroe the Star
Player: top winning
dog, 1991.
            Trafford.

of the Congo in 1960, and then to Firelight of the Congo in 1961. The first litter included two tricolours, indicating that one or more of Fula's forebears must have been tricolour. Consolation received his tri genes from Eng. Am. Ch. Black Ace of the Congo (his great grandfather).

A litter born in 1964, line-bred back to Fula, from Ch. Fulafuture of the Congo and Fulastar of the Congo produced a hitherto unknown colour, which appeared to be black/white at birth, but after a few weeks tan hairs appeared on the cheeks, behind the ears and behind the tail. With maturity, this colour tends to have an invasion of tan hairs mingling with the black body colour producing a 'sabling' effect, and tan 'spectacles' may be produced. There are no 'melon pips' above the eyes. This colour became known as 'Fula Black' or recessive black. The colour black/tan and white, as distinct from black/tan and white with mask and melon pips, was added to the English Standard in 1986. Since its first appearance the colour has become prevalent, occurring particularly in matings which are line-bred to Fula of the Congo. The top winning tricolour at the present time, with ten CCs, is Ch. Horsleys Sirsarah, owned by Mrs S. Higgitt.

In 1975 Jack Fleming (Niangara), Miss Doris De-Leeuw and a Mr Corrigan, a gentleman who knew the country well, journeyed to the Sudan in search of native dogs. They acquired two dogs, but due to internal politics and an excess of red tape, they were unable to bring them out of the Sudan. The dogs were left in care of friends in Juba for onward transmission when conditions improved, but unfortunately they were never allowed to leave Africa.

Former Basenji breeders who have contributed a great deal to the present-day Basenji, either by having been in the breed before 1950 or having bred at least one English Champion include:

Andersley Mrs E. G. Anderson.
Antefaa Miss D. Willans.
Bambuti. Mrs Nicholson.
Basbox Mr J. Eachus.
Basenlake Mrs J. G. Goodman.
Belbraq Mrs H. Howe.
Blackpits Mr L. Siddall.
Blean Mrs O. Burn.
Buckiebrae Dr A. Mackenzie.
Cookshall Mrs P. Kent.
Congo Miss V. Tudor Williams.
Courtlands Mrs C. Graham.
Curlicue Mrs D. Bergwall.
Cutmill Mrs C. Ward.
Dennysmoor Mr J. Malcolm.
Downhatherly Mr H. Hopper.
Dormtiki Mrs G. White.
Drumabas Mrs M. Bowden.
Dunnerdale Mrs M. Dilley.
Fianna Mrs A. Lait.
Gooses Miss C. Campbell.
Houndsmark Mrs M. Field.
Janhillbry Mrs Moss.
Kingsway Mrs K. Russell.
Kunetown Mrs W. Pearson.

Lasgarn Messrs Edwards.
Lionslair Mrs M. Brown.
Lograk Mr & Mrs Kargol.
Littlebreach Mrs I. Percival.
Maibridge Miss D. Howis.
Mochi Mrs M. Gallacher.
Niangara Mr J. Fleming.
Nimshi Miss Lawrence.
Ousefleet Mrs L-Emerson.
Pilon Cmdr & Miss Bishop.
Redesgarth Miss M. Herring.
Ridingsgold Mrs C. Tress.
Riviana Mrs P. Cook.
Roina Mr R. Thackrah.
Sunnyshane Mrs F. Roberts.
Silvercaul Mr W. J. Kent.
Sin Miss D. Berry.
Snowkobi Miss K. Wells.
Syngefield Mr & Mrs Williams.
Tancor Mrs Shepherd.
Thomastown Mrs Lewarn.
Whitewood Mr B. R-Frost.
Windymead Miss E. Gardner.
Zapotec Mrs G. Coutt.

Present-day affix holders who have produced one or more English Champions are:

Abazinja Mr & Mrs Castellani.
Adoram Mr M. Quinney.
Azenda Miss M. Christy Davies.
Benjalah Mrs J. Goodman.
Bokoto Mr & Mrs J. Horner.
Bubas Mrs J. Anderson.
Dassita Mrs C. Wright.
Domewood Mrs E. Bowers.
Emmzar Mrs C. Bradley.
Horsleys Mrs Wilson Stringer.

Ijnesab Mrs S. Bateman.
Ituri Mrs J. J. Browne.
Jisgard Mr A. Gray.
Khufu Mrs K. Marszalek.
Neyeliz Mr & Mrs S. Smith.
St Erme Mrs St.E. Cardew.
Taysenji Mrs E. Ford.
Tenki Misses Juniper.
Zande Mr & Mrs Wallis.
Zizunga Mrs I. Terry.

New exhibitors and breeders are joining the breed all the time and will probably be the well-known names of the future. Mr and Mrs Smith's Ch. Neyeliz Cascade, was retired from the show ring in 1987, and became the Top Stud dog in 1991. His daughter, Ch. Ijnesab Bedazzled at Jethard, owned by Paul Singleton and John Taylor, is top winning bitch, and a grandson, Salvadori's Ch. McEnroe the Star Player is the top winning dog of 1991.

Chapter Eight

THE BASENJI
IN NORTH AMERICA

THE FIRST IMPORTS

The very first Basenji to arrive in the New World was a stuffed one – complete with hunting bell – featured in the African Pygmy Group exhibition, conceived by Herbert Lang and Dr Chapin and shown in the American Museum of Natural History from 1909-1915. In 1956 Dr Chapin, who had become intrigued by the breed while setting up the exhibition, went back to Africa to obtain a Basenji, called Tiki Tiki, from the pygmies of the Ituri Forest. It was hoped that Tiki Tiki would contribute towards the good of the breed in America. An article in the *New York Times* of 25th January 1958 shows a picture of Tiki Tiki, and states that he was sent to Bettina Belmont Ward's kennels in Middleburg, Virginia. There has not been any further mention of him, so it would appear that the American Kennel Club would not grant studbook registration.

In 1937 three Basenjis arrived in New York aboard the *SS Berengaria.* They had been bought from Olivia Burn in England by Mr and Mrs Byron Rogers, who became interested in the breed after its debut at Crufts of that year. The dog, Bakuma of Blean, was of direct African extraction, having being sent to the United States straight from English quarantine. The two bitches, Basashi and Rougie, were bred in England, under the Blean prefix. Unfortunately the two bitches, and a litter born to one of them, all died. Bakuma was given away to a good home, subsequently rediscovered in 1940 by Alexander and Mary Phemister, and renamed and registered as Phemisters Bois. There is not much doubt that they were the same dog, as old photographs show the two dogs to have identical markings.

In 1941 a stowaway dog was found on a freighter, the *West Leshaway*, docking at Boston with a cargo of coffee beans on its return to the United States from a West African port. (Olivia Burn also used to travel on this ship on her journeys to and from the Congo.) This little bitch, which had survived for more than three weeks without food and only such water as she could acquire from licking condensation from the sides of the hold, was in a pitiful state when she was found. She was looked after by the Animal Rescue League of Boston.

Following press coverage of the story, Mr Phemister (a noted Obedience trainer of that time – he once trained an English Bulldog to CDX standard) went to see her. She was almost all-white, with brindle on her ears, a brindle patch on her right side and a docked tail, but he pronounced

*A stuffed Basenji –
the first to arrive
in the New World –
exhibited in the
American Museum
of Natural History,
1909-1915.*

G. Gilkey.

*Tiki Tiki: this
Basenji was
obtained by Dr
Chapin from the
pygmies of the
Ituri Forest in
Africa.*

her to be a Basenji. (While I was in Africa I was told that the natives in Gambia and Sierra Leone used to dock their Basenjis' tails so that their prey, gorillas, could not get a hold on the dog and rip them apart.) This Basenji bitch was named Phemister's Congo and she was duly mated to Koodoo of the Congo, a dog Mr Phemister had obtained from Dr Richmond in Canada. A dog from the resulting litter of three was Phemister's Barrie, who in 1942 became the first Basenji to win an obedience Companion Dog title.

George L. Gilkey owned one of the first Basenjis in America when he bought a puppy, sired by Kookoo of the Congo out of Kiteve of the Congo, from Dr Richmond in June 1941. Mr Gilkey's Basenji was Tanya of Windrush, the foundation bitch of the Rhosenji kennels. At the first Basenji Specialty show Mr Gilkey took Best of Breed with Ch. Rhosenji's Beau and Best Opposite Sex with Ch. Rhosenji's Ginger. Mr Gilkey also imported Wayfarer of the Congo, a brother to Widgeon of the Congo, who had been sent from England to Mrs Anderson in Canada.

These two were sired by Wau of the Congo, but did not carry three-generation UK registration, and so Wayfarer could not be registered by the AKC. However, he obtained a 'listing', which enabled him to be shown. He gained enough points for his American Championship, although the AKC would not give him a Championship certificate. The Canadian Kennel Club also refused to register him – although they had accepted his sister – because he had been refused by the AKC. Wayfarer is reported to have been on the large size, with good movement. Unfortunately his many good breed points were never utilised, as there is no record of him ever siring a litter.

In 1941 Kindu and Kasenyi (originally named Congo and Libra) arrived in the United States with a shipment of gorillas. It was said that five puppies had been born to them on the voyage, and that there was one other dog. However, the pups and dog did not survive. Mr Gilkey confirms these details in an article he wrote in one of the first copies of *The Basenji*. Penny Inan researched and wrote the following report for the Northern Californian Club Specialty in 1981 at the request of the Club Chairman, Margaret Sommer.

"In 1941 a consignment of gorillas arrived in New York by ship with two unusual passengers aboard. They were Basenjis, one male and one female, later known as Kindu and Kasenyi. The gorillas were imported by Henry Trefflich, a wild animal importer; the dogs had been placed aboard the ship by Mr Carroll, an employee of Mr Trefflich. Mr Carroll had seen Basenjis in the French Congo and thought perhaps American fanciers would be interested in this unusual breed. He had originally collected eleven dogs to be shipped but just prior to sailing seven of the dogs escaped and only these two survived the voyage. Mr Trefflich exhibited the dogs at the 1942 Westminster Kennel Club Show under the names of 'Congo' and 'Libra' and they appeared on a poster taken from a portrait by James Montgomery Flagg.

"The two were unwanted by Eastern Basenji fanciers, according to Walter Philo, as they were quite different from the dogs imported from England – considerably smaller and more compact. (Kindu – then called Congo – was reportedly 14" square). Since he had been unable to place them in the East, Mr Trefflich sent them out to Goebel's Wild Animal Farm in Thousand Oaks, California.

(Note: These two dogs were probably smaller than the dogs imported from England; however, the size differential was quite probably due to their being direct African imports. Amatangazig of the Congo was 14$\frac{1}{2}$ inches tall and Fula of the Congo was 15 inches. The subsequent generations of imported dogs tended to be more towards our current size range.)

Phemister's Congo, the stowaway found on board the West Lessaway, 1941.

Coco of the Congo (Kinga of the Congo – Zandia of the Congo). Bred by Veronica Tudor Williams, imported by George Gilkey, Wisconsin, USA.

Wayfarer of the Congo, owned by George Gilkey. This Basenji was not eligible for AKC registration, although his sister was registered in Canada.

"John Taaffe of San Anselmo, California became interested in the breed and contacted Mr Trefflich for further information. He referred her to the two imports at the Animal Farm. Tess Taaffe was at that time a breeder of Gordon Setters under the kennel name of Martinero, and was later approved to judge sporting breeds, Afghan Hounds, Beagles, Bloodhounds, Norwegian Elkhounds and Basenjis. In March 1943 Mrs Taaffe purchased the two dogs and renamed the male 'Kindu' and the female 'Kasenyi'. It appears that she did not exhibit Kasenyi, possibly as she was reportedly an older dog, but showed Kindu at Golden Gate's Show, with attendant publicity on the "Barkless Dog from Africa". She sent him to New York in 1945 where he was placed first in the Miscellaneous Class under Alva Rosenberg, and later he took four Bests of Breed at Californian shows. In July of 1945 Kindu was placed second in the Hound Group under judge Derek Rayne.

Kindu and Kasenyi: this pair of Basenjis arrived in New York with a shipment of gorillas.

Kindu and Kasenyi appeared on the cover of *Western Kennel World Magazine* in February 1946 and an advertisement inside offers one female and four male puppies, sired by Kindu out of Kasenyi, whelped December 10th 1945. The males were 250 dollars apiece and the female was 350 dollars. Although this was the third litter they had produced for Mrs Taaffe, it was the only one registered. (They may also have had a litter – either on shipboard, or shortly after arriving in New York which did not survive; I was unable to verify this.) Kindu and Kasenyi were individually registered in April 1946; both were listed as having been born in 1940, with Mrs Taaffe as the owner. Kindu was described as 'tan and white' and Kasenyi as 'chestnut and white'.

"The puppies in the litter were all registered as 'chestnut and white', in May 1946. Their names were Kasenyo (for the bitch), Kingolo, Kindulo, Kinsuto, and Kintoto – all owned by Mrs Taaffe. Following the death of John Taaffe (a prominent criminal attorney), his wife sold Kindu and Kasenyi to Helene and Lyle Vaughan of Koko Crater kennels in Hawaii. The pair produced another litter on January 5th 1947, from which only one puppy was registered, a male, Akamai of Koko Crater, chestnut and white. Kindu was killed by a car and Kasenyi died of old age, but I was unable to get any further specifics.

"Prior to the move to Hawaii, Kindu was bred to two other bitches. On November 26th 1945, Gayety of Sirrah Crest whelped a litter from which three were registered: Kindu of How Gert, male, fawn with white markings; Baria of Kin-Gay, female, fawn with white markings, and Bombo of Kin-Gay, male, registered as 'black'. A litter out of Safari, bred by Frank Gorsuch, was whelped May 6th 1946. Two dogs were registered from this litter: Bandundu, male, dark red fawn with white markings and Safari's Puella, female, chestnut with white markings. Of the offspring of Kindu and Kasenyi (including Kindu's two other litters) only four had litters registered in the studbook. Ch. Kingolo is behind many great breeding programs and kennels on both sides of the Atlantic. Together with his sister Kasenyo, he produced a litter of seven for Hallwyre Kennels (Forest Hall), many of whom finished their titles.

"Kindulo was the only other one of that first registered litter to produce registered offspring. He was purchased by Koko Crater Kennels and together with his younger brother, Akamai of Koko Crater, he produced a line of dogs ancestral to the kennels of Rancho Rest, Ter-senji, Story Book and Khajah. The first Best in Show Basenji in the United States (in Hawaii) was Philo's Blaze of Koko Crater, sired by Akamai of Koko Crater, out of a Kindulo daughter – with Akamai of Koko Crater as a great grandsire on the dam's side.

"In the course of my search for information on Kindu, Kasenyi and their owner, Tress Taaffe, I have compiled some personal comments from people who knew Mrs Taaffe and Kindu (Kasenyi apparently spent her time at home with puppies). According to Eleanor Bird, the dog was capable of quite a scream, and caused problems with Mrs Taaffe's neighbours. When I contacted Juliet Rosemount Trissel and asked if she had known Tress Taaffe, she replied that she had known her so well that at one show Mrs Trissell sneaked up and slipped the lead off Tress's dog, carrying it away (as a joke). And the dog – you guessed it – was Kindu.

"She describes his temperament as friendly with those he knew, standoffish with those he didn't. He was fine in the ring, but didn't really like having his mouth looked at. She explained that he had a coat similar to a Smooth Fox terrier, very close and a very good rust color like that on a Doberman Pinscher. She also remembered him having a very good tail. Derek Rayne remembered placing Kindu in the group, but unfortunately was not able to give me a specific critique of the one dog. He mentioned that 'the breed was not as elegant as they are today.' He also noticed 'the improvement in gait since that time', but noted 'the breed is often lacking in wrinkles and/or breed expression.' He remembers 'the earlier dogs were seldom tricolors – mostly red with less white than today.' The movement lacked 'the drive of today's dogs'. He finds 'that the Basenji is one of the few breeds that overall has improved since...(he has) been judging 40 plus years.' "

The Basenji Club of America was formed in 1942 with Alexander Phemister as President, George E. Richards as Secretary; Treasurer George L Gilkey, and Vice Presidents, Ethelwyn Harrison and Dr Eloise Gerry. Basenjis were admitted to the Studbook in 1943, under the same Breed Standard as the 1942 English version. There were fifty-nine registrations in the first few months and by 1945 the one hundred required for the breed to be classified in the Hound Group had been achieved.

The Roscoe B. Jackson Memorial Laboratory at Bar Harbour, Maine has had a colony of Basenjis since Dr Gerry provided the Laboratory with the original pair in 1945 and 1946. These were Jinga, born 1942, by Can. Ch. Kwillo of the Congo out of Juliana of Windrush, and Rosemary of Windrush, born 1941, by Koodoo of the Congo out of Kwango of the Congo. All the Basenjis at Bar Harbour are descended from this pair. "Physically they are not very good show types by modern standards, but they resemble the pictures of Basenjis taken in Africa, being rather long-bodied, rangy animals." So wrote Damara Bolte in an article printed in 1960.

The Basenjis at Bar Harbour are studied to provide information on coat colour, seasonal breeding, barklessness and fertility. Considerable research is also being conducted into the Basenjis' dislike of restraint and the fact that Basenji puppies display more initial fear in strange situations than do puppies of other breeds.

AM. CH. KINGOLO
Kingolo, one of the puppies of the first Kindu-Kasenji litter went to Mr Forest Hall of Hallwyre

Am. Ch. Kingolo: one of the first puppies from a Kindu – Kasenji mating. He won his title in 1951.

kennels, and he won his American title in 1949. In 1951 when he was six years old he was sent to the Syngefield Kennels of Richard and Sylvia Williams in Ireland. The following article was written by Walter Philo in 1958:

"Am. Ch. Kingolo is now twelve years old, and there are some as might say that he is getting old and broken, but in truth, he looks wonderful with hardly a grey hair on his head, and him everyday studying the world with dark, quizzical eyes. The Irish mist being what it is and rolling in from the sea and over the countryside constantly, he has long suffered from a bronchial cough, which has grown worse with the passing of time only because he has learned to indulge it to invite admiration. Standing all of sixteen inches Kingolo wears a coat of deep smouldering red and of softest texture, with a waistcoat of white, a white stocking on his right front leg and a white sock on his left.

"A judge would take note that his back feet are white, his nose coal-black and his tail double curled tight, and also might say that soundness and stamina are there. Kingolo's is the type of head that surely one would expect to see peering worriedly from the equatorial bush at the brave white hunter as he goes about decimating what is left of Africa's wild species. 'Dreamer', as he is known, has a will of iron and there is no power on earth that will move him from a door if he knows that Sylvia Williams is on the other side.

" 'He adores me and I, him', she writes, 'so that we do each other's ego the world of good. Having been a kennel dog until he came to Syngefield, he quickly realized that he had fallen on his feet in a big way, and has never looked back or had occasion for regret. From the vast depth of nigh on twelve years living with Basenjis, I have never yet come across another like Dreamer. Honest and reliable, he is a great lover of the simple things in life. He is never nasty to other dogs and he is always charming to people. He is worshipped by all his children and grandchildren, and he plays like a puppy with them and with us.

"There is another side of the coin, however, otherwise he would be just a dull paragon. He considers himself a mere lad, has absolutely no dignity and never looks where he is going. When complimented on his fine appearance, he still performs his little dance which consists of the movement of a bucking bronco, all the while bobbing and bowing to the right and the left endlessly. This he learned a long time ago in the great state of Texas where he spent his youth.'

"The son of a pair of French Congolese Basenjis that had come straight from Africa to the United States in 1941, Kingolo, as a pup, was acquired by Forest N. Hall. In 1947 and 1948 – years when the fabulous Mr Hall was breeding and exhibiting Basenjis instead of only judging them – Kingolo made twelve appearances in the show rings of the Southwest, going BOB every time and placing six times in Group under Cassleman, Ferguson, Vary, Kendrick, Harris and Muir. In 1948 he was Best of Breed at Westminster and in 1949 returned to Madison Square Gardens to repeat this achievement, while in 1950 Ch. Kingolo's Kan Kan carried on the fine tradition of his old man.

"When he was six years old Ch. Kingolo went to Eire to take over from the J. R. Williamses the mastership of Syngefield in Birr, which, as you know, is in County Offaly. According to my notebooks, Kingolo has been the only American Basenji ever to emigrate to the old country, where he is considered part of the foundation stock. Mrs Williams feeling that it would be unjust to expect him at his age to compete with the juvenile mashers parading up and down the show rings, he was shown in England not at all, and only at a few Irish shows.

"Although he has been used very little at stud, either side of the Atlantic, he has sired fourteen Champions – one or more in each of his litters. He won the Stud Dog Cup offered by the Basenji Club of Great Britain for the dog whose progeny won the most points in English shows in 1952/3, 1953/4 and 1956/7. In 1955/56 the cup went to his son, Ch. Pongo of the Congo. A list of Kingolo's top winning grandchildren and great-grandchildren – English, Irish, Canadian and American – would fairly run off the bottom of this page and there is hardly a Basenji being shown today, anywhere, that does not have his name in its pedigree.

" 'Apart from all he has done,' concludes Mrs Williams, 'Dreamer is still the most adored Basenji in the whole world. Words cannot express our feeling for him. He is 22 carat all the way through and has given us all the happiness and fulfilment that any dog could give to man. It is no wonder therefore, that any scion of Kingolo's going forth into the world, leaves Syngefield only after a solemn pledge from the new owner that it shall not live in a kennel and never shall it be sent away from those it has learned to love. It is a matter of opinion whether a man might traffic in dogs as in worldly goods, but it would be indeed a poor man and a sorry one that would be trading in the humanities.'

"A well known English judge of that time, McDonald Daly, reported on Kingolo that 'he did not like his head as it lacked wrinkle and expression, the rest, lay of shoulder, body, legs, feet etc. were excellent, as a sire he stamped his offspring with his excellent body yet permitted his pups to retain the more captivating expressions of the dam.' "

In the early 1950s Leo Shadic, another Basenji enthusiast, who was for many years Treasurer of the BCOA, imported Eng. Ch. Vagabond of the Congo. He is pictured in Miss Tudor Williams' book holding a handful of Champions: Int. Ch. Vagabond of the Congo, Am. Ch. Phemister's Golden Dawn, Am. Ch. Black Tulip of the Congo, Am. Ch. Verbena of the Congo and Am. Ch. Phemister's Mainstay.

THE BETTINA KENNELS
A newspaper cutting from *The Washington Post and Times Herald* dated Thursday 24th 1955, by

Kitty Slater, gives the following account of the Bettina Kennels:

"Basenjis, one of the oldest and yet one of the newest canine breeds, are coming into fashion in the hunt country of Virginia. The barkless dogs, recently publicised in the bestseller *Goodbye My Lady* (now being filmed into a movie production with Brandon deWilde as the child star) have their present Virginia headquarters at the kennels of Bettina Belmont Ward, near Middlesburg. Mrs Ward, whose husband, Newell J. Ward Jr, is Master of the Fox Hounds of the Middlesburg Hunt, divides her sporting interests between foxhunting and the breeding of those rare African hunting dogs, who have been noted for grace, beauty and intelligence since the days of the Egyptian Pharoahs.

"Her introduction to Basenjis was in the winter of 1952/53 when the Ward family, including two very small fry, Danny and Daphne, were on a foxhunting junket in Ireland. Due to the quarantine law no pets from their Newmary Farm could be taken along and Bettina said she couldn't face all that time without a dog. Having heard of the remarkable barkless breed, she cabled ahead to a kennel in England and her first Basenji was on hand to welcome the family at their rented place in County Limerick, Ireland. She immediately became charmed by her new-found pet and her deep interest in the breed was quick aborning and has been fast abiding.

"Bettina Belmont Ward's Basenjis are from the best possible bloodlines and her parent stock was handpicked with great care from Veronica Tudor Williams' Congo kennels in England and the Syngefield kennels in Ireland. She has at stud Ch. Gold Pip of the Congo (whose granddaughter will be in the aforementioned motion picture) and his first American litter has produced, among other winners, Bettina's Bronze Star. The latter, when eight months old, went Best of Winners at one of the largest shows on record in the US for Basenjis, at Lackawanna in August 1955.

"In addition to these two stud dogs, Mrs Ward also has at her Middlesburg kennels, Champion Brahme of Syngefield who at nine months achieved his Championship with five Best of Breeds and one Best Opposite Sex. 'Boomer' did a great deal to popularize the breed at the time, with his charming, out-going personality, when temperament in the breed was generally poor. At the Rockcliffe show in 1955 a bitch, named Riviana Jollity of the Congo, won Best of Breed and finished her Championship after only being exhibited at five shows. This in dogdom is quite a feat but not much really for the Royal Basenji." (Jollity was the first Champion to be sired by the African-imported Wau of the Congo.)

'GOODBYE MY LADY'

During wartime in 1942, Veronica Tudor Williams received a heavily censored letter from James Street telling her about his stories *Weep No More My Lady* and the sequel *Please Come Home My Lady*, which were published under the title of *Goodbye My Lady*. The story as first published in the *Saturday Evening Post* was illustrated with a painting of Tanya of Windrush, a bitch bred from two 'of the Congo' dogs by Dr Richmond in Canada, and owned by George Gilkey of the Rhosenji Kennels. In the 1950s Warner Bros made a film of the book, with Brandon deWilde, then aged thirteen, as the lead.

"This film created great interest in the breed and it is now available on a Warner Bros video. Miss Tudor Williams was asked to send a dog to play the role of 'Lady', and a bitch, My Lady of the Congo, was shipped over from England. After the film was finished, Brandon deWilde kept My Lady as a family pet. Miss Tudor Williams was also requested to send over 'doubles', and these included Flageolet, My Love and My Lord of the Congo. In all, there were seventeen 'doubles' present during filming, the others being bought or leased from American breeders.

Sheila Anderson of the Glenairley kennels, engaged as a consultant on the film, took Flageolet of the Congo back to Canada at the end of filming. He later became an American and Canadian Champion, and the sire of twenty-four Champions. Mrs Bettina Ward obtained My Love of the Congo, who later went to Bob Mankey's Cambria kennels. When she was mated to the tricolour Ch. Bettina's Oryx, she produced that well-known tricolour, Ch. Cambria's Ti Mungai, who became the sire of fifty-two American Champions. He was, for many years, the top winning tricolour until he was beaten in 1981 by Barbara and Carlos Jimenez's Ch. Arabrac's Mountain Mamba. Ti Mungai, along with Bob's foundation dog, Ch Phemister's Kedar, really put Basenjis and Cambria kennels on the map in California. In partnership with Jack Schafer, Cambria continued to be a force to be reckoned with in the show ring until Bob's death in 1987.

DEVELOPMENT OF THE BREED

The 1950s saw many well-known kennel names coming to the fore. Mary McWain of the Haku Kennels bought Black Idol of the Congo in 1947. Sadly Black Idol died of leptospirosis when within two points of her title. Mrs McWain's next imports, Eng. Ch. Black Ace and his litter sister, Black Mist of the Congo, smooth-coated, well-marked, black tricolours, took Winners Dog and Winners Bitch at the first BCOA Specialty in 1950. Norm and Mae Wallace of Tinas Coma Kennels bought in Ch. Glenairley Black Munia, bred by Sheila Anderson from her imported Wau bitch, Widgeon of the Congo, as their foundation stud. Damara Bolte had been kennel manager at the Bettina kennels from 1955 to 1958, and in October 1958 she bred the first Reveille litter (what could be a better prefix for a military family?) from her foundation bitch, Ch. Bettina's Fedha.

One of the puppies was Ch. Reveille Rifleman who, in his only litter before his early death, sired Ch. Reveille Recruit. Recruit was an outstanding dog: he won one hundred and twelve BOBs and sixty-four Group placements, and had twenty-nine champions to his credit. A mating of the imported dog, Fula Reveille of the Congo, to a Recruit daughter, Ch. Rose Bay's Gay Buta, produced six males and one female, namely Ch. Reveille Ruffles of Rose Bay. When she was mated back to Recruit and Recruit's sons, Ruffles was Top Producing Basenji Dam in 1971.

A puppy born to Ruffles and Recruit was Ch. Reveille Re-Up who won one hundred and forty Best of Breeds at All Breeds Shows, sixty Group wins, including one at Westminster (the only Basenji to do so) and is the sire of eighty-five Champions, holding second place in the Stud Dog Honour Roll. During 1962 Lepper's Nik Nak won three Best in Show awards. In 1964 the Zande Kennels held top spot with Ch. Feruzi of the Zande, owned by Ross Newmann, of the Betsy Ross kennels, winning thirty-six BOBs.

In 1959 the Marlise Kennels of Gt Barrington, Mass. were sent a Liberian-bred black and white Basenji, which passed through English quarantine kennels and while there was passed for Class 2 Kennel Club registration by a well-known judge of that time, Leo Wilson. Following the arrival of Whizz in the United States, Elizabeth Ryder was so impressed by the bitch's temperament that she went to Liberia and brought back several Basenjis. It would appear that the AKC did not register these native-born dogs as nothing more was heard of them.

Towards the end of the 1960s Gwen Stanich of Coptokin kennels imported black and white Basenjis from Bert Blewett in South Africa. The dam of these dogs was Coptokin Copper Bikini. The first black and white Hound Group One winner was Ch. Bushveld Black Shikari, in 1973. Shirley Chambers of Khajah kennels imported Sir Datar of Horsley, a young black and white

Ch. Arabrac's Mountain Mamba, owned by Carlos and Barbara Jimenez.

descendant from Satin and Sheen, who had been sent earlier to the Horsley kennels. Datar had three generations English Kennel Club registration behind him, so was now eligible for registration by the American Kennel Club. From the same litter Sir Dannitar went to Marvin Wallis' Zande Kennels and a bitch Sirdollytar also arrived in the United States. The top winning American black and white is Ch. Black Power of Woz, a grandson of Ch. Sir Datar of Horsley – his record includes four First in Group in 1973.

The 1960s also saw the arrival in America of the third generation offspring of Fula of the Congo, the little native bitch that Veronica Tudor Williams had taken back to England from the Sudan. These early imports gave a great deal to the American Basenjis and were widely used in breeding programmes, mostly with great success, although not all breeders were enamoured with the new stock. One outstanding dog that resulted from a mating of Ch. Fulaflashi of the Congo with Ch. Reveille Recruit was Ch. Kajah's Gay Flambeau of Ed-Jo, who went on to sire fifty-nine Champions. Another well-known early owner and breeder was Phyllis Elliot of Ka and Ba Basenjis.

Breeders and exhibitors already active in Basenjis in 1970 included Al Braun of Henty P'Kenya (famous hunting Basenjis); Robert House (Anubis); Carol Webb (Kazor); Dee and Jeri Crandall (Delahi); Melody Russell (Fanfare); Cecelia Wozniak (Woz); Iris Craven (Kasai); Susan Kamen-Mariscano (Apu); Shirley Jones (Hoo); Deanne Lehu (Lihu); Russell Hendren (Asari); and Mel and Maxine Stringer (Marabasi). Coming on the scene in the 1970s were: Midge Greenlee (Serengeti); Mary Lou Kenworthy (Kenset); Jon and Vicki Curby (Kibushi); John and Margaret Sommer (Rameses Basenjis of VII); June Young (Changa); Mike Work (Sirius); Barbara and Carlos Jimenez (Arabrac); Patricia Edgerton (Edgie's); Jane Williams (Candu); Joanie Hunter (Tizamba); Andie Paysinger (Pendragon); Diane Coleman (Absinthe); Jon and Susan Coe (Akuaba); Mary Watkins (Libra); Chuck and Judy Milton (Edrosembe); Sally

*Ch. Sukari Steven Speilbark,
bred by Kathie Jones.*

*Ch. Shadowbye's Mitty,
owned by Lannis Kircus.*

*Ch. Shadowbye's
General Business,
owned by Loretta
Kelly.*

Wuornos and Patricia Bright (Sonbar); Betty White (Akili); Sandy Bridges and Penny Inam (Jato); Chuck Bagnell (Kenobi); and Sheila Smith (Anasazi). Starting out in the 1980s were: Judy Secaur (Fantasia); the Hacker family (Hacker's); Stella Sapios (Astarte); Julie Jones (Jasiri); Kathie Jones (Sukari); Nancy Black (Kiburi); Pat Cembura (Arubmec); Ken and Marylin Leighton (Zuri) and George and Terri Gavaletz (Bushbabies).

The 1970-80s saw the emergence of such names as Ch. Shadowbye's Mitty (owned by Lannis Kircus) holding top spot in the Stud Dog Honor Roll with 100 Champions and Ch. Shadowbye's General Business (owned by Loretta Kelly). The All Breed Best in Show winner, Ch. Camp's Dazzling Nazimba (owned by Barbara Camp), the tricolour Ch. Arabrac's Mountain Mamba (owned and bred by Barbara and Carlos Jimenez), the Leighton's Ch. Rameses Golden Phoenix, Ch. Aleika-Absinthe Rajah's JR (owned by Janice and James Wessman), Pat Cembura's Ch. Arubmec's The Victor, Ch. Vikentor's Country Rose (owned by Judy Cunningham) which was the Number One Basenji in 1990. The BOB winner at the 1990 BCOA Specialty was Mrs Symington's Ch. Serengeti Reveille Larkspur, handled by Damara Bolte, and in 1991 the winner was Ch. Sonbar's Celestial Wizard, bred by Sally Wuornos and Patricia Bright. There are many other breeders deserving mention for their contribution to the breed, and I apologise to any that I have not included.

RETURN TO AFRICA

Because the original Basenji gene pool in England and America was so small, several American breeders, concerned by the growing health problems that this factor was creating in the breed, felt it was essential for the future welfare of the Basenji outside Africa that an effort should be made to obtain more African-bred animals and have these accepted into the AKC Studbook. There were several questions to be answered before embarking on a safari. Did Basenjis still exist in Africa as pure bred? Would Basenji breeders in America and the world accept native types, which would undoubtedly vary considerably from the home-bred ones, selected over the years to conform to the Breed Standard? Finally, could the American Kennel Club be persuaded to register new imports?

In February 1987 Jon Curby (a past president of the BCOA) and Mike Work of Sirius Basenjis with their guide, John Valk, went to the Garamba Park, which lies along the Sudanese-Zaire border, to look for the Azande tribe and their Basenjis. Travel in Africa, especially in the more remote, backward regions is extremely slow. Tarred roads are unknown; there are just dirt tracks through the bush with pot-holes the size of trucks, which are passable with a vehicle in the dry season but a nightmare of mud and water in the rains. The 180 miles from an overnight stop in Isiro to Garamba Park took eight hours to cover. In an article published in *The Basenji* in November 1988 Jon Curby wrote:

"It is interesting that the edge of the Azande area and the beginning of the open savannah coincide. The obvious reason would be that Azande hunting techniques do not work in open grassland. The use of Basenjis and nets in the tall grass would be futile. The Azande prefer to set up a series of nets of about 333 meters total length in a horse-shoe shape in the forest area. They usually leave the nets in place for a day or two before using the Basenjis to drive the game into the enclosure to be trapped in the nets and speared." They also saw what Veronica Tudor Williams had once described as "mahogany tri-color". Jon writes that "the best comparison he can make is to a red Doberman except with the typical Basenji white points. We saw several Basenjis with this coloration and found them to be quite attractive".

Ch. Aleika Absinthe Rajah's JR: seven times Best in Show winner. Owned by Janice and James Wessman.

Ch. Arubmec's The Victor, owned by Pat Cembura.

The party continued towards Doruma. Jon Curby continues: "After driving for some hours on some of the worst roads we had seen, we came upon a group of hunters. There were six or seven older men each carrying a spear and machete, and most of them had large woven hunting nets over their shoulders. Most interesting to us was the Basenji hunting dog with them. It was a beautiful brindle male, complete with hunting bell. He did not like the look of us and tried to stay just out of sight in the forest, but we could hear his bell as he moved around behind the hunters. After a while John learned from the owner of the brindle dog that he had a female puppy sired by his dog, that was about eight weeks old.

"He was not interested in selling her, but we told John we HAD to have her, even though we had no idea what she looked like. John convinced the hunter that we would pay enough for him to buy three puppies, so he agreed to get her for us. We waited for about twenty minutes while the puppy's owner went to his home in the bush to retrieve her. She was a very small, pest-ridden, almost black brindle thing of about six weeks of age. By this time we were accustomed to seeing puppies that were dehydrated and malnourished. We, therefore, ignored her round head, big ears and rat-like tail, knowing that at some point she would turn into a "normal" looking Basenji."

Ch. Sonbar's Celestial Wizard, owned by Sally Wuornos and Patricia Bright.

Seven Basenjis were brought back to the United States from this expedition: three females – a brindle and two reds; and four males – two tricolours, one red and one brindle. In March of the following year Jon Curby, Stan Carter, a veterinarian and a long-time Basenji breeder, and Damara Bolte of the Reveille Basenjis, went to Haute Zaire (previously the Belgian Congo). Once again John Valk was their guide. Damara Bolte wrote an article in the *American Kennel Gazette* in September 1988:

"The dogs we saw were in surprisingly good condition considering their resident fleas and worms and their nicks and scratches. Puppies are weaned very young, dams having little milk to give. The adult dogs fend for themselves and are generally in good shape. These native dogs live symbiotically with their masters: each part of the other's life. They share the fire, the hut, the hunt and the food. Although we saw little petting of dogs, there is a strong bond between man and dog."

"The colour variants intrigued us, most notably the tiger striped brindle (Miss Tudor Williams wrote enthusiastically of the brindle colour, stating that it was a true African colour and that the Basenji Club was dedicated to preserving the breed as it is in Africa. Although she was on the board of the Basenji Club of Great Britain and seemed to be pro tiger striped brindle she did not explain why this colour was excluded). We saw a grizzle colour with tan mask, as seen in Salukis and many of what in Corgis are called red-headed tris. There were individuals of all three colours, red, brindle and tri, open marked with white.

"From what we could learn through our interpreter the natives made no effort to mate a bitch to a special dog. Our selection of puppies was limited to what was available. We wanted pups about eight to ten weeks old and did find five that appealed to us, from five different litters and from different areas. Two were tri males, one a lightly brindled male and two were red bitches. The sixth, from a very remote area, a lovely tiger striped brindle bitch, may be seven months old.

Avongara M'Bliki: designated as foundation stock.   Damara Bolte.

Avongara Elly: Winners Bitch and Best Opposite Sex at the Woodstock and District Canine Show in Canada, 1990.

However, our last acquisition might be the jackpot, a red bitch in whelp. She is of excellent type with a super curled tail and the dam of two handsome yearling sons. After several hours of bumping contentedly along on the back seat she gave birth the next morning to six puppies. Time – and the conscientious and cooperative efforts of dedicated breeders – will tell if these individuals from Haute Zaire will make a positive contribution to the future of Basenjis."

In June 1990 the native-born Basenjis were registered with the AKC. Designated as foundation stock, they may be bred from and exhibited. Thirteen animals were registered, all with the prefix Avongara (the clan from which all Azende Chiefs are chosen), with which all pure-bred African stock will be designated. There were two brindle males, Diagba and Gangura and two brindle females, Bazingbi and M'Bliki; two tricolour males, Wele and Nabodio; one red male, Renzi; and six red females, Zamee, N'Gondi, N'Gola, Kposi, Goldi and Elly. All the dogs had been health and eye-screened, all were clear of any known Basenji ailments; seven showed minor P.P.M. in the eye tests. In 1990 Avongara Elly won Winners Bitch and Best opposite Sex at the

A representative of fourth generation stock, bred down from Pygmy Esenjo.

Kibushi Get Sirius, sire of the first brindle Champion, owned by Michael Work and Jon Curby.

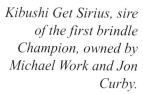

Ch. Changa Ashanti Sana Bakavua: the first brindle Champion, owned by Michael Work and Alyce Alexman.

Ch. Changa's Hot Damm Here I Am: the second brindle Champion, owned by Tracie Gramann and June Young.

Ch. Akuba on the Wild Side: the first African-bred red/white Champion, made up in 1992, owned by Susan Coe.

Woodstock and District Canine Association show in Canada under judge Jose Payro.

In June 1983 Margaret Sommer of Rameses Basenjis of VII kennels was contacted by a gentleman requesting the use of one of her stud dogs. He explained that he owned a native-born bitch, bred by the pygmies of the Ituri Forest, which had been given to him as a 'thank you' gift for providing them with meat during a time of drought. He had a veterinary export permit from Zaire in his possession as corroboration of his story. Mrs Sommer knew that neither the bitch nor any of the resulting puppies could be registered with the AKC under the regulations then in force, but she took the opportunity of having the bitch, Esenjo, confirmed as being typical of the breed by Penny Inan, Sandie Bridges, Doreen Duffin (Australia) and myself as the UK representative.

Doreen and I were both in America at the time on judging assignments. Margaret felt that it would be a sin not to take advantage of this once in a lifetime opportunity of obtaining pure, new African blood for the breed, so Esenjo was mated to Rameses Tut-Ankhamen, a grandson of Eng. Ch. Fula Friend and Ch. Fula Nefertiti, both 'of the Congo', and therefore closely line-bred to native stock, i.e. Fula of the Congo. There were four puppies in the resulting litter. Unfortunately, Esenjo's owner died before he could see them, but the Sommers took the litter to rear in an environment as close to their natural habitat as possible.

At the time the Avongara Basenjis were accepted in the studbook, Esenjo and her puppies were registered as well. Margaret Sommer has now bred down to the fourth generation. The first Championship to a brindle Basenji was awarded in 1991 when Changa's Ashanti Sana Bakavua, owned by Alyce Alexman and Michael Work, was made up, followed very quickly by the success of her brother, Changa Hot Damm Here I Am, owned by Tracie Gramann and June Young – both from a litter bred by June Young. The first half African-bred red and white Champion was made up in May 1992 – Ch. Akuaba on the Wild Side, owned by Susan Coe and bred by Susan Coe and D. J. Blake, sired by Avongara Renzie and Ch. Jocasta JR on Parade.

CANADA

THE FIRST IMPORTS
Canada is certainly a land of 'firsts' where Basenjis are concerned. In 1939 Dr Andrew Richmond of the Windrush Kennels bought Kowboi and Kokombo of the Congo from Miss Tudor Williams, but unfortunately they both died from distemper shortly after their arrival. Kowboi was subsequently stuffed and put on exhibition in the Royal Ontario Museum. In 1940, following the death of the two imports, Dr Richmond acquired Kiteve, Kikuyo, Kwillo and Koodoo, all 'of the Congo'. These dogs were exhibited at the Morris and Essex Show in 1941 and created great interest. Kiteve and Kikuyo were females, Kwillo and Koodoo were males. In 1943 Dr Andrew Richmond became the owner of the first Basenji Champion in the world when Kwillo of the Congo obtained his Canadian title.

At a show in Toronto in 1947 there was a Basenji entered belonging to Mr and Mrs Keegan; this was Ping of the Congo. The Keegans had brought Ping and Yei of the Congo back to Canada from England. In 1951 Can. Ch. Akabaru of the Blue Nile, Ping's grandson, recorded the first Basenji Group win at Toronto where he was the only Basenji entered. Akabaru was owned by Roberta Jenkins, bred by Mary McWain. In 1953 he went on to win his American Championship, thus becoming the first dual Can. Am. Champion.

In 1949 Sheila Anderson returned to Canada after a stay in Hong Kong, bringing home with her a dog from Magician of the Congo and Lotus of the Congo, one of a litter bred while she was residing in the colony. That dog was to become Can. Ch. Joss of Glenairley Can. CD, the first show and obedience titled Basenji in the province. His son, Am. Can. Ch. Glenairleys Black Trellis, a tricolour, eventually became the first dog of that colour to win a Group in Canada. As if these honours were not enough, Mrs Anderson had also imported Eng. Ch. Orange Fizz of the Congo from Miss Tudor Williams; Orange Fizz gained her Canadian Championship to add to her English one, thus becoming the first dual Eng. Can. Champion.

1954 saw the arrival of Widgeon of the Congo, imported by Sheila Anderson to provide much needed new blood for the breed. Widgeon was the daughter of the African-bred Wau of the Congo and Frivolity of the Congo. Miss Tudor Williams described Wau as being "built like an

*Am. Can. Ch.
Dainty Dancer of
Glenairley: the first
Canadian Basenji to
win an All Breeds
Best in Show.*

Arab horse with a wonderful neck and shoulder and long graceful legs. His hindquarters are faultless. He has the proud carriage and springy walk we wish to preserve in the breed." In an article printed in *The Basenji* in 1976 Mrs Anderson relates that when she first saw Widgeon she was rather surprised: "Widgeon was a little brown dog, with very little wrinkle, hardly any curl, a very heavy coat, no elegance at all. However, she did have a well proportioned head with a short muzzle, her ears were small and well set on top of her head, her eyes were almond shaped and deep brown, a well set tail (but little curl), a short back and correct angulation, hocks well let down with good feet. She was also a sweet, sensible, utterly adorable little dog."

Her first litter to Can. Am. Ch. Glenairley Black Trellis produced seven puppies including Glenairley Missalthrush, who became grandmother of Dainty Dancer of Glenairley, and a tricolour dog, Merlin, who holds a record for obedience work with a score of 199 out of a 200 at the Bremerton Obedience Trial in 1957. At the time that Widgeon arrived in Canada, the Canadian Kennel Club accepted for registration all dogs holding an English Kennel Club registration. Mr Gilkey in the United States, who had bought Widgeon's brother, Wayfarer, was not so fortunate, as the American Kennel Club would not register the dog, because he was from African-bred stock and did not hold a three-generation registered pedigree. Wayfarer, although tall, was a most elegant, typey Basenji whose use could have benefited the breed.

INFLUENTIAL BREEDERS

In 1956 Margot Bowden bred a litter from which Margaret Robertson of Merlea Kennels picked out a little bitch, who was to become the very well-known Am. Can. Dainty Dancer of Glenairley. On the way to becoming a dual Champion, Dainty was the first Canadian Basenji to win a Canadian All Breeds Best in Show – this was achieved at the tender age of nine months. It seemed that her record would never be broken as she amassed seven Best in Shows in Canada and the United States, eighteen Group Firsts and numerous Best of Breeds. But in 1979 Am. Can. Ch. Nordayl's Daily Double, bred by D. Neveu and owned by Larry Kunz, was Top Basenji 1978 and '79. Placed in ninth place in the Hound Group in 1978, Daily Double overtook Dainty Dancer with sixty-one Breed wins and thirty-five Group placings.

In 1962 Mrs Bowden and four of her Drumadoon Basenjis came to England, settling in the

Am. Can. Feliji of the Zande: winner of twenty-eight BOBs.

Ch. Hadrian of Basenlake: Number One Canadian Basenji in 1966.

Anne Roslin Williams.

Can. Ber. Ch. Spearwood Tirzah, Best in Show winner 1973, owned by Cheryl Egerton.

Ch. Conamore's Follow T'Sun: Top Basenji, 1976.

Am. Can. Ch. Conamore's Sun and Jasmine: Best in Show, 1989.

New Forest area. The English Kennel Club would not allow her to use her Canadian prefix 'Drumadoon', so all her English litters were registered as "Drumabas". She stayed in the New Forest until 1973, pursuing a successful show and breeding programme. Many of the resulting puppies were exported back to Canada, Australia and the United States. She returned to Canada in 1972, but unfortunately ill health forced her to retire from the Basenji scene.

Am. Can. Ch. Asali of the Zande, bred by Marvin Wallis, who is still breeding and showing Basenjis in England under the Zande prefix, held the Canadian Number One spot in 1959 and 1960. The same breeder also held the top position in 1961 and 1962 with Am. Can. Ch. Chafya of the Zande, and in 1964 Am. Can. Ch. Feliji of the Congo was top Basenji and held tenth place in the Top Ten Hounds with twenty-eight BOBs. 1965 saw the arrival from England of Eng. Ch. Hadrian of Basenlake, bred by Ernest Goodman, who became Number One Canadian Basenji in 1966 and gained his American and Canadian titles.

In 1968 Am. Can. Bermudan Ch. Zambesi Sparkle, owned by Donna Spencer and Mr Vix, was Number One Basenji and fourth of all hounds. In 1973 a great-granddaughter of Dainty Dancer once again won an All Breed Best in Show for a Canadian Basenji; this was Can. Ber. Ch. Spearwood Tirzah, owned and shown by Cheryl Egerton. She went on to be the foundation bitch for the Conamore Kennels. One of her well-known descendants was Am. Can. Ch. Conamore's Sun and Jasmine, who became only the second Canadian Basenji to win more than one All Breed Best in Show. She was Top Basenji in 1987/88 and /89, with six All Breed Best in Shows and a BCOA National Specialty Best of Breed.

1976 was the year that Ch. Conamore's Follow T'Sun was Top Basenji and placed fifth in the Top Ten Hound list. To Marnie Lang goes the honour of being the only breeder-owner-handler of Group One winning Basenjis in all three colours recognized at that time, namely: Am. Can. Ch. Shantara's Blactamb Solar Scene (black and white), Am. Can. Ch. Shantara's Gentaa

Snowdancer CD (red and white) and Can. Ch. Shantara's Dalaf Thunderbolt (tricolour). Thunderbolt was a grandson of Solar Scene, a son of Snowdancer and the first non Canadian-bred Basenji Best in Show winner.

The original Canadian Basenji Club was founded in August 1964, with Margaret E. Robertson as President. When that club was wound up, Cheryl Egerton wrote to all Canadian Basenji owners, and with the help of Christine Kempster the club was reformed in 1989 with a membership of over one hundred. The first BCOA National was held soon after the formation of the new club, with Am. Can. Ch. Changa's Slick of Conamore winning Best of Breed. The second Specialty was won by John Donald's Am. Can. Ch. Barhu's Kudabin a Flirt, who has also won a Canadian Best in Show. She is currently a contender for a placing in the Top Ten Hounds.

Malcolm MacDonald, a founder member of the original Basenji Club, imported Fula Princess of the Congo, and possibly the first black and white to be brought into Canada – Sir Donitar of Horsley. Mr MacDonald Obedience trained his Basenjis. His tricolour dog, Ch. Merlea Ebony Mubaku Can. Am. CD, and his son, also a tricolour (from Fula Princess of the Congo), namely Ch. Benji Tricop Ebony Kayunga CD, were excellent ambassadors for the breed in the obedience ring in the sixties.

During the Eighties top Basenji positions were held by Nancy Keen's Tagati Kennels, with Am. Can. Ber. Ch. Tagati Chimo's Brigadoon Bride holding the top Basenji spot in 1985 and '86. The Karush kennels of Pam and Ray Roy did the same with Ch. Karush Kel Khalil Ben Kala in 1983 and '84. The dedication and work of so many past and present Canadian breeders is now coming to fruition with numerous Basenjis gaining top honours in Groups and Best in Shows.

Chapter Nine

BASENJIS AROUND
THE WORLD

AUSTRALIA AND NEW ZEALAND

THE JUDGING SYSTEM

As Australia is so vast, each State has its own Kennel Club and Shows run under its own rules. This is now altering – all States have now adopted an universal judging system under the auspices of the Australian National Kennel control, and the show system is slowly being changed to run on a uniform basis. At the present time all States follow one Breed Standard, the English version, although there are talks being held about following the Breed Standards of the country of origin in the future – this may cause some problems in the case of Basenjis!

The method of awarding Championship status is the same throughout the country. To become a Champion, a dog has to earn a 100 points, which are only won at Championship Shows. These are allotted as follows: five points plus one point for each exhibit of that breed and sex. Thus, if there are four dogs and seven bitches, the dog CC winner will get nine points and the bitch CC winner will get twelve points. Best of Breed does not entitle the exhibit to any more points. However, if the Best of Breed winner goes on to win Best Exhibit in the Group, it would then get a maximum of twenty-five points – the points won at breed level are not counted; twenty-five points is the maximum that can be won at any show, even when the breed has an entry exceeding that number. Therefore, a dog could become a Champion in four shows by winning four twenty-five points, either at breed level or by winning the Group. These four CCs must be won under four different judges. Judges are encouraged to withhold the CC from exhibits they do not consider worthy of becoming a Champion.

QUARANTINE RESTRICTIONS

In the early years, dogs that were sent to Australia from England had to suffer a three month sea voyage, and then a further three months quarantine on arrival. With the advent of a regular flight service things became a great deal easier, and in 1973 these quarantine laws were relaxed so that dogs were permitted to fly to Australia and then undergo three months in an Australian quarantine kennel. Dogs from America are obliged to spent six months in English quarantine,

Bronze Wing of Clendon: one of the early Basenjis in New Zealand.

and then a further six months residency in England before continuing their journey. However, quarantine laws have recently changed, and the Australian quarantine period for a dog from England is now sixty days. A dog from America still has to spend six months in English quarantine, but it can then enter Australia for a further ninety days quarantine, without undergoing the English residency requirement. American dogs can come through Hawaii, and the same conditions apply.

THE FIRST IMPORTS
The honour of bringing the first Basenji to Australia belongs to the late Dr Lex Caselberg of Wollongong, New South Wales – a Great Dane breeder. He was reading an article on Danes from England when a marker fell out, which had some information about Basenjis printed on it. Dr Caselberg and his wife became fascinated by the breed, and in 1948 they imported Fanfare and Cocotte of the Congo from Veronica Tudor Williams. These were closely followed by Andersley Aurora, from Mrs Anderson, and in 1948 the first Basenji litter was born, with Fanfare and Cocotte as the parents – both having become Australian Champions. In 1950 the first tricolours arrived – Black Night and Black Pearl of the Congo – litter sisters sent out by Miss Tudor Williams to Dr Caselberg, who bred under the Danecourt prefix. By 1951 he owned more than twenty Basenjis. Black Knight became an Australian Champion and Black Pearl went

to New Zealand.

Mrs Cormack, of Victoria, also became interested in the breed, and in 1949 she imported Maibridge Careless and Maibridge Bunty, from Miss Howis of England. In 1950 a litter was whelped under the 'Altahalach' prefix.The four years 1949-1953 saw Basenjis being exhibited at Australia's premier shows, Melbourne and Sydney Royal; but when Dr Caselberg became ill in 1953 his dogs were placed in good homes with owners who did not have much enthusiasm for showing or breeding, and the breed declined to such an extent that no Basenjis were bred in Australia during the years 1957-1960. It looked as if the breed had disappeared 'down under', but fortunately New Zealand enthusiasts ensured their survival in this part of the world.

Earlier imports from Australia included Black Pearl of the Congo, Altahalach Zeppo and Danecourt Rae. Rae was in whelp to Ch. Fanfare of the Congo, and this produced the Cimbri strain for Dr Hope-Pearson. A mating of Cimbri Claudius and Cimbri Chloe produced Pinecroft Sally, later a Champion, who became the foundation bitch of Mrs Dawn Clark's famous 'Of Clendon' Basenjis. Dawn Clark imported Andersley Brownchad Velveta in whelp to her sire, Ch. Andersley Atlantic, from the UK. Mrs Boot ('Of Jordan' Basenjis) imported Iago and Marietta of Littlebreach, and these names are at the back of many Australian pedigrees.

THE SIXTIES

Mrs Beryl Hancock moved to Australia from New Zealand, and in 1960 she imported NZ Ch. My Lady of Clendon (later to become Aus. Ch.) and Red Pride of Clendon. She then moved from Melbourne to Sydney, where she met Miss Janine Outram who had an imported tricolour – Black Satin of Snowkobi – bred in England by Mrs Kay Wells. There was now breeding stock to keep the breed alive in Australia. Further imports from New Zealand followed: Whim-a-Way of Jordan to Mrs Kneipp; Portia, Cherie and NZ Ch. Lovely Lady of Clendon to Lillian and Keith Barker.

In 1965 several dogs were imported from the UK. Fula Kiwi of the Congo went to Dawn Clark in New Zealand, and his litter brother, Fula Zuki, together with Riviana Angachifi and Riviana Frolic, went to Mrs Betty Arthur in Melbourne. The following year Crystal Silk of Clendon was imported by Alan and Lauris Hunt, and Gold Corduroy of Clendon was imported by Bill and Win Chandler, and this put Basenjis on a solid foundation for future breeding.

During the next few years imports were plentiful, both from New Zealand and the UK. Tenki Fula Toucan of the Congo went to Mrs Delma Clatworthy in Brisbane, Fula Phantom of the Congo went to the Barkers, and Fula Black Witch of the Congo went to the Chandlers. The first of four American imports now arrived. Kotikokura of Kigoma came with his owners, Paul and Shirley Neal, to settle in the country. In 1968 the bitch that was to have such a great effect on the breed was imported from Canada by the Barkers, namely Drumadoon Dark Dainty, bred by Mrs Margot Bowden. Dainty produced fifteen Champions from four litters, and she is behind many of the country's top winners.

THE SEVENTIES

A rabies outbreak in England in the mid-sixties resulted in a ban on all importations, but in 1971 the first black/white in the country arrived to the Hunts in Sydney – Horsleys Sir Frasertar – along with Eng. Ch. Sirclarencia of Horsley, who was to become the first Eng. Aus. Champion in the world. Both were bred by Mrs Wilson Stringer. Sir Frasertar produced the first black/white Australian-bred Champion with the Hunts' Pukkanut Tallawong. The Hunts also owned Aus.

Ch. Pukkanut Wyvern: the only black/white Basenji in the world to go Best in Show at an All Breeds Championship show.

Trafford.

Eng. Ch. Kingsway Penny Petite, imported from England.

Anne Roslin Williams.

Ch. Pukkanut Wyvern, the only black/white Basenji to go Best in Show at an All Breed Championship show. Ray and Judy Harper brought in another black/white, Horsleys Sir Frumfreetar, and a tricolour, Horsleys Sirfunygirl. Several of the Drumabas (previously Drumadoon) breeding also arrived around this time.

During the early seventies, New Zealand breeders were also importing Basenjis from England, among them four Horsleys, three St Ermes, bred by Mirrie Cardew, including Eng. Ch. St Erme Painted Pony, and two bred by Kath Russell – a tricolour, Kingsway Sea Anemone, and Eng. Ch. Kingsway Penny Petite. Bazendax Jungle Bunny also found her way out to the Land of the Long White Cloud, going to Paul and Peggy Whincop, where she became a NZ Champion. Many New Zealand Basenjis went to Australia and Tasmania, including animals from Impala, Jordan, Clendon, Karnak and Osiris kennels.

LATER IMPORTS

Later imports to arrive were: Domewood the Artful Dodger, sent from 'Bunty' Bowers to Ron and Doreen Duffin in Melbourne; Panderville's Dinkie Doll sent from Peter Yallop also to the Duffins; Eng. Ch. Horsleys Sirgeorgina to Mrs Jackie Coulson in Melbourne; Eng. Ch. Horsleys Sir Hugo and Horsleys Sir Hecuba to Freda Snell and Jenny Craig in North Queensland; Domewood Delinquent to Dorothy and Marylin Oestreich in Brisbane; and Dormtiki Softly So Softly and Dormtiki Makuba Nairi to Delma Clatworthy in Brisbane. In 1986 Azenda Dream Maker was sent from Margaret Christy Davies to Helen and Larry Keenan in Sydney.

Further imports from America also arrived. Am. Ch. Touch O'Class of Woz, bred by Cecilia Wozniak, went to the 'Tamsala Kennels' partnership of Jan Robert and Audrey DeLittle; 'Caddi' became the first Am. Aus. Ch, and very nearly gained his English title, winning two CCs during his six months residential quarantine in England. Other imports to the Tamsala Kennels were Reveille Red White and Blue, True Blue of Woz, Am. Ch. Prince Charming of Woz and Three Wishes of Woz. A further American import has recently arrived in Sydney – Khamsin Bound for Botany Bay, going to Sophie and Angela Tromp. Quite a few of the imported dogs have gone on to obtain their Australian Championship titles; several have been Best in Hound Group winners, and in 1975, Domewood the Artful Dodger (by now an Australian Champion) became the first Basenji to go Best in Show at an All Breeds Championship in Victoria. He was also a Basenji Specialty Best in Show winner.

AUSTRALIAN EXPORTS

The trade was not all one way. Australian dogs have been exported to New Zealand, America, Canada, England, Denmark, Sweden, Finland and Singapore, and have made their mark in their new homes. Aus. Ch. Afrika Royal Challenge was sent from Marie and Frank Dymock's Afrika kennels to Veronica Tudor Williams, where 'of the Congo' was added to his name, and he rapidly gained his English Championship. He sired top winning show dogs, and was top stud dog in 1985 and 1988. In total, he won seven CCs. Afrika Royal Tradition went to the Asari kennels, owned by Russell Hendren in California, and another Afrika dog went to Hawaii. Over the years many Australian Basenjis have been sent to the United States, beginning many years ago when Hazel Brownlee sent a dog to Bob Mankey. They are now too numerous to mention, but among the best known was Aus. Ch. Balshah Allakazam, who was sent originally to Canada and then moved to the United States where, in the ownership of Penny Inam and Russell Hendren, he became the only Australian dog of any breed to obtain his Field Championship.

Am. Ch. Touch O'Class of Woz, bred by Cecilia Wozniak in America, imported by Tamsala Kennels.

Aus. Ch. Domewood the Artful Dodger: the first Basenji Best in Show winner at an All Breeds Championship Show in Victoria.

Am. Can. Hagunn Sudan: the first Australian Basenji to gain dual Championship.

Eng. Aus. Ch. Afrika Royal Challenge of the Congo: winner of seven CCs in England.

Aus. Ch. Balshah Allakazam: exported to Canada and then the United States, where he became a Field Champion.

Vicky Cook Photography.

Ch. Jebelmarra Hiperno, owned by Ross and Kay Eldred.

Ch. Baagna Justa Fella: winner of six Best in Show awards.

Ch. Baagna Lyka Hussy, a daughter of 'Fella', and a prolific winner in her own right.

The Tamsala kennels exported Aus. Ch. Tamsala the Blue Kondor to the US, where, handled by Damara Bolte, she won Reserve Bitch at Westminster – America's most prestigious show – and another Australian-bred bitch, Am. Aus. Ch. Kasai Shukarani, owned by Kathy Hansch, won Best of Winners and Best Opposite Sex at this show in 1985.

Shukarani, and several other Basenjis, moved to the United States with Kathy and Lindsay Hansch when Lindsay was posted to the Australian Embassy in Washington for three years. When Beth Canavan moved to the US she took several Azande dogs with her. The Duffins sent Makuba Am Masari to California in 1985, and more recently, Makuba Kito Sheela was sent to Finland. In 1990 the Hunts sent back to England a descendant of their original black/white import, Horsleys Sir Frasertar. This was Aus. Ch. Pukkanut Night Music, and she whelped four puppies while in quarantine; the sire was Aus. Ch. Pukkanut Hello Darkness.

Australian registration rules prohibit the addition of a prefix, an affix or an additional name, once that dog has been initially registered. The breeder's prefix must be the first word in the name and no other breeder's prefix can be added, regardless of whether the dog is an import or not. Thus it can be seen at a glance who bred a dog, and as there is no other breeder's prefix included, there can be no confusion as to who is actually the breeder. A person or partnership can also register their names as a 'kennel', as in 'Tamsala Kennels', therefore all the dogs they breed will have 'Tamsala Kennels' listed as the breeder's name, and not individual names.

THE BIG WINNERS

Australia has, according to many famous international judges, including Veronica Tudor Williams, the late Bobby James and Rainer Vourinen from Finland, produced the some of best Basenjis in the world. Amongst these great dogs are: Ch. Wandra Midas, Ch. Wandra Blue Nile, Ch. Wandra Inca Goddess, Ch. Wandra Bronze Fantasy, Ch. Wandra Midian, Ch. Wandra Goddess Nardia and Ch. Wandra Ti Mungai, all bred by Lillian and Keith Barker. Lillian was the founder of the Basenji Club of Victoria, and during the years that they were breeding, the Barkers produced over fifty Champions. Other famous Basenjis include: Ch. Abadan Kamili Binamark, bred by Nance and Frank Anderson; the Dymocks' Ch. Afrika Little Tiger, Ch. Afrika the Westerner, Ch Afrika Ima Tigress (owned by Val Innes), Ch. Afrika Ambassador, Ch Afrika Masterpiece, Ch Afrika Masterly and Afrika Dubonnet, who gained her place in history when she won Best Opposite Sex and Best Puppy in Show at the 1976 Sydney Royal Easter Show – the second largest show in the Southern Hemisphere. Following this success Dubonnet was not shown again.

Marie and Frank Dymock and their son, Glen, have been very successful in the breed in Australia, with many home-bred Champions to their name. Ch. Pukkanut Wyvern and Ch. Pukkanut Tallawong (the first Australian-bred black/white bitch Champion) won many awards for Lauris and Alan Hunt, as did Ch. Jebelmarra El Berber, Ch. Jebelmarra Hiperno and Ch. Jebelmarra the Jester, for Ross and Kay Eldred. 'The Jester' was dog CC winner and Best in Show under Damara Bolte at the 1st Australian National Specialty in 1985; the previous week he had won the dog CC and runner-up BOB under Robert Cole at the famous NSW Spring Fair.

During recent years, John Forbes has had outstanding success with his Ch. Baagna Justa Fella. 'Fella' won six Best in Show awards (All Breed, Hound and Specialty Shows) in New South Wales, including Best in Show at the Canberra Royal Show. He retired with over 1500 Championship points to his credit. His litter sisters, Ch. Baagna Just a Doll and Ch. Baagna Justa Honey were also outstanding winners. That super litter was sired by Ch. Makuba Al Simba out

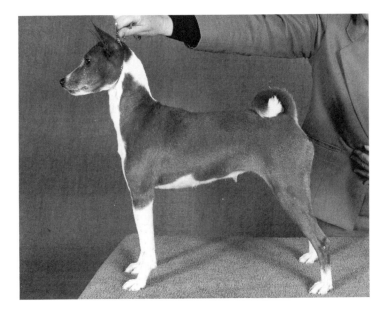

Ch. Makuba Am Mbindi: winner of three Melbourne BOB awards.

Ch. Makumba Al Amba: winner of the Bitch CC and Best Opposite Sex at the first Australian Specialty.

Photography by Twigg.

of Ch. Baagna Golden Style. Fella's daughter, Ch. Baagna Lyka Hussy, is another prolific winner, with a Specialty BIS to her credit and over 1000 challenge points in three years. John has been in the breed since 1974, and he has bred thirty-six Champions to date.

Another great winning dog, who retired with over 1500 CC points, was Merle and Peter Burn's Ch. Jambazi Akili, sired by Ch. Domewood the Artful Dodger. Akili made history when he became the youngest Basenji to win a Best in Show at an All Breeds Show in Australia at eight and a half months old. In Victoria, one of the truly great dogs was Ch. Pharoah Red Sirocco, bred by Ray and Judy Harper and owned by Mrs Jackie Coulson. He has the distinction of

*Ch. Tengku
Naini: Best in
Show winner,
1988.*

*Photography
by Twigg.*

*Ch. Helios
Rocky Royale,
bred by Denise
Doyle, winner
of two Specialty
Best in Show
awards.*

winning five Melbourne Royal Challenge Certificates.

   The Melbourne Royal Show is the largest and most important show in the Southern Hemisphere, and dogs come from all over Australia to exhibit there. Only one Basenji has ever won a major award at the show, and that was Mick Lindsay's Makuba Am Mbindi when she won Best Opposite Sex in the Hound Group (about 1000 hounds) in 1985. She also won three Melbourne Best of Breed awards – the last at six years of age. The Duffins' Ch. Makuba Al

Amba won four Best Opposite Sex awards at All Breed Championship Shows, Royal and Basenji Specialty Challenges, Best of Breed at the NSW Spring Fair, under Robert Cole of Canada, and Bitch CC and Best Opposite Sex at the First Australian National Specialty, judged by Damara Bolte. She retired from the ring with about 1000 Challenge points, in spite of taking time out to produce three litters. Her dam, Makala Gizelle (bred by Dorothy Oestreich of Brisbane) was another prolific winner, winning CCs at three Specialty shows in different States and Best in Show at the New South Wales Specialty under the late Bobby James, from England.

Joan McGrory's home-bred Ch. Akrabu Jinja, a great showgirl, holds a record six Specialty Challenges in the three states of New South Wales, Victoria and South Australia, and won Best of Breed at three of them. She was Best in Show under Veronica Tudor Williams, as was her dam, Ch. Risregor Regal Dalabu (bred by Tasma Place) during Veronica's first visit. Dalabu also notched up a very impressive show record. A daughter of Jinga, Ch. Akrabu Tudor Rose was the bitch CC winner at the 1984 Victorian Specialty, and in 1985 she became the second Basenji to win a Best in Show at an All Breeds Show in Victoria. The first to win this honour was the Duffins' import, Ch. Domewood The Artful Dodger in 1975. In 1988 Ch. Tengku Naini (bred by Mick Lindsay) also hit the top spot, followed three years later by Tamsala Kennels' Ch. California Gold, who has been a great winner for Tamsala. This is equally true of Ch. Tamsala Tan Ariki, twice Best in Show at Basenji Specialities, and Ch. Tamsala Calico Patches. Their recent import, Am. Aus. Ch. Prince Charming of Woz, has also been very successful in the show ring, winning the dog CC at the NSW Specialty in 1991.

Denise Doyle's home-bred Ch. Helios Rocky Royale has been another prolific winner, with two Specialty Best in Show awards – one of them under Harry Needham of Scotland. Past dogs that come to mind are Beth Canavan's Ch. Azande The Zulu, who has the distinction of being first Best Exhibit in Hound Group winner back in February 1972; the Harpers' Ch. Pharoah Tri Pekoe and Ch. Pharoah Black Panther (owned by Jan Robert), the first black/white dog Champion in Australia; Jan Roberts' Ch. Tamaiti Tahi Tinawha and Ch. Tamaiti Tahi Teina; Richard and Jan Bricknall's Ch. Janir Afro Tomtom and Tamsala Kennels' Ch. Tamsala Blue Sancerre and Ch. Tamsala the Bluekondor (exp. USA).

TASMANIA

A dog bred by Denise Doyle, Ch. Helios Pepsi Cola, went to Eileen and Stan Laycock in Tasmania, and made history in 1987 by becoming the first Basenji Best in Show winner in that State. Tasmania does not have a large population, so Basenji breeders are few and far between. However, the Laycocks with the Eilsta prefix, have kept the flag flying in the island for many years. In Queensland, Dorothy Oestreich's Ch. Makala Eagle Hawk was a great winner (including BIS at the record 200 entry NSW Specialty in 1976, as was his dam, Ch. Makala Bahr El Ghazal.

Another of the well-known Makala dogs was Ch. Makala Equaliser. Sheila Corbett's Ch. Micyn Kisumu Majuba (bred by M. and C. Collett) was one of Queensland's top Basenjis, with many Group and Best in Show awards, and at nine years of age she won the CC at Brisbane Royal, plus Reserve CC under Damara Bolte in 1985. Juba, who died aged fifteen, really was a great Basenji. Louise Marsden's Ch. Lomar Chardonnae was another successful bitch with a NSW Specialty to her credit. Queensland and New South Wales have had many winners at Best in Show level, particularly in North Queensland, where Freda Snell (Farelyn) and Jennie Craig (Zaire) have been showing for many years.

SOUTH AUSTRALIA

In South Australia, the Bambuti kennel, owned by Pat Gupelle, has been responsible for keeping the breed to the fore, especially with Ch. Bambuti Gorgeous George, who won Best in the Hound Group at two Adelaide Royal Shows. Mary Ball and Nita Stunnell are also longtime breeders of Basenjis in the State.

WESTERN AUSTRALIA

Although far distanced from the Eastern States, Western Australia has still managed to have an impressive Basenji population. Beth Swallow's Myola kennels, Inge Gregory's Basongo kennels, along with Elizabeth and Jim Jackson's Debrak kennels, keep the flag flying there.

THE NORTHERN TERRITORY

The Northern Territory, with such a small human population, also has its Basenji fanciers in Rick and Jan Van Der Velde in Darwin. They have been successful over the years with Basenjis in Obedience, as have the Dwyers in Canberra.

Specialty shows are only held by the Victorian and New South Wales Basenji Clubs, as the clubs in other States are social clubs only, which may hold Competitions and Matches but not Open or Championship Shows. South Australia used to hold Specialties, but when their Basenji population dwindled they were unable to hold their annual Championship Show.

Adapted from 'The Growth of Basenjis in Australia', presented to the 1st National Basenji Conference held in 1985 by Doreen Duffin , updated by Mrs Duffin in 1992.

SCANDINAVIA

FINLAND

This country has the fourth largest Basenji population after America, Australia and Britain. The original import from Sweden was Bal Dek a red/white dog, owned by Doris Loflund. Bal Dek had a Norwegian female companion in the following year, a tricolour, Black Penny of Rossanty. Unfortunately both these animals were of uncertain temperament, and there was only one litter bred. Of the resulting puppies a bitch, Penny, was mated to Hely Sudqvist-Masalins' English import, Int. Nordic Ch. Janhillbry Bala, who was the first Finnish Basenji to win Best in Show – an honour he achieved twice in 1967.

In 1965 Fula Finn and Fula Flon Flon of the Congo were imported to Marti Korkia-Aho. Over the next eight years, nineteen puppies were born, but only seven were shown with any regularity. These first imports had very little effect on future breeding. Fula Farm Girl of the Congo, imported by Helga Kauste, and Fula Goldraisin of the Congo, belonging to Seppo Jauro, arrived in 1972. Goldraisin also won a Group and became an International Champion, as did Fula Farm Girl. English imports now arrived in quick succession. Azenda Gilt Edge, a tricolour, in whelp to Ch. Hubert of Houndsmark, went to Kirsti Kolvu. Two years later she bought Azenda Flying High, bred by Margaret Christy Davies; Fula Softly of Dormtiki, bred by Hebe White, went to Marja Ojal Karki. These dogs made excellent foundation stock for Finnish Basenjis.

Int. Nord. Ch.
Fula Farm of
the Congo.

Int. Nord. Ch.
Azenda Gilt
Edge.

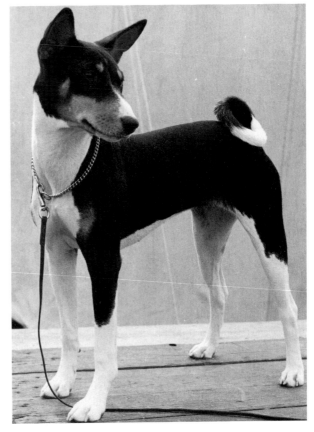

*Int. Dk. N. S. SF
Ch. World
Winner 89
Silentium
Faida.*

*Int. Nord. Ch.
Azenda Flying
High.*

By the end of 1976 there were 81 Basenjis in the country, rising to 180 in 1982, with an entry of around 25-30 dogs at the larger shows. In 1985 Andrew Thompson (England) had an entry of 50 Basenjis at a Specialty Show; this entry was beaten in 1992 when Margaret Christy Davies had a record 68 dogs. At this show Best of Breed was awarded the title winner for 1992 – this was Visakoivun Winnie The Pooh. Best in Show was Furahan Ikela.

The Finnish Kennel Club was founded in 1972, and from the beginning they have had a skilled breeding committee of Hans Lehtinen, Ranier Vourinen, and recently Mrs Marja Talvitie, who with the breeders give advice on proposed breedings and assess the current puppies and new

*Int. Nord. Ch.
Janhillbry Bala.*

*Dk SF Ch WW-89,
KPHW-89
Sternhimmels Es
War Einmal.*

imports. Those that do not reach the required standard are banned from any breeding programme, thus ensuring the maintenance of the high level attained by Finnish-bred stock. To date, the most important females in the country have been: Int. Nord. Ch. Fula Farm Girl of the Congo, Int. Nord. Ch. Azenda Gilt Edge, SF. S. Ch. Uulan Blacksara, and Int. Nord. Dk. Ch. World Winner 1989 Silentium Faida, born 1984. Males who contributed most to the breed include: Int. Nord. Ch. Winner 1978 Azenda Full Of It (an import from Sweden, who sired two successful litters with Fula Farm Girl of the Congo), Int. Nord. Ch. Winner 1976 /1977 Azenda Flying High, and Int. Nord. Ch. Winner 1987 Feidias, born in 1982. These Basenjis have all had an important influence in Finnish Basenji history

Several Finnish Basenjis have become All Breed Best in Show winners: Int. Nord. Ch.

Int. Nord. Ch.
Winner 1986
Kidoko.

Dk SF Ch,
JWW-89,W-89,
EuW-91 Azenda
Dreamtime.

Janhillbry Bala, at Hyvinkaa and Porvo in 1967; Int. Nord. Ch. Winner 1986 Kidoko succeeded three times in 1986, at Kaivoksela, Helsinki and Kotka; EuJunWinner 1991 Kenzongo's Kinongo, at Hameenlinna; and SF Ch. EuWinner 1991 Sternhimmels Gerd Gepard, in Vantaa. The Copenhagen World Winners for 1989 were: Sternhimmels Es War Einmal; Azenda Dreamtime and Silentium Faida, who also won the Progeny Group at the European Winner Show in Helsinki in 1991, when Brenda Banbury (England) was the judge. At the Helsinki Show EuJunWinner 1991 Best of Breed was Kenzango's Kinongo, in second was EuJunWinner 1991 Azenda All Is Well, third was EuWinner 1991 Sternhimmels Gerd Gepard, and in fourth was EuWinner 1991 BOS, Azenda Dreamtime.

The Finnish Basenji Club has members from Sweden, England and Australia, all of whom

Swed. Ch. Gobbo of Littlebreach.

Swed. Ch. Lilli.

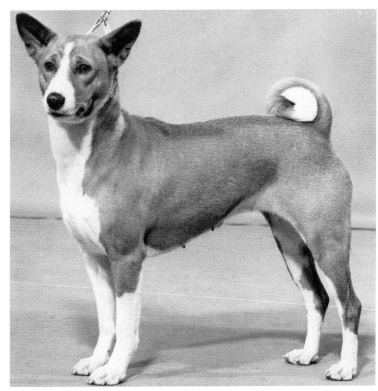

Swed. Ch. Pythia.

Int. Nord. Ch.
Azens Full Of It
(with his 3,000-
year-old
Egyptian
ancestor).

receive the Club magazine translated into their own language. Finnish Basenjis are seen at most Scandinavian and European Shows among the top dogs, and are doing a great deal to promote the breed.

SWEDEN
The first Basenjis in Sweden were bought by Diana Bergwall of Christmas Kennels in 1951. They were Fop, Flower and Flirt of the Congo. Fop and Flirt went on to become Nordic Champions. In 1952 Mrs Bergwall brought Flower and Flirt back to England, where she continued to breed under the Curlicue affix, until her last KC registered litter of eight puppies in 1958. While still in Sweden Mrs Bergwall sold puppies to Mona Gotman and Irma Hardsell. Irma later imported Swed. Ch. Gobbo of Littlebreach from Mrs Percival. Gobbo proved to be a very important import, siring three bitch puppies in three different litters. These puppies were responsible for four Basenji enthusiasts, who are still active in the breed at the present time.

One of the puppies was S. Ch. Lilli, owned by Mia Lowbeer and her sister Monica Massih, who also owned Pansy of Rossanty. Lady MacBeth went to Elisabet Selinus of Senjisfinx kennels, and Swed. Ch. Pythia became the property of Karin Gabrielson. Elisabet Selinus then imported Nord. Ch. Fulaspiki of the Congo. Unfortunately her line was lost so she brought in S. N. Ch. Azenda Fula Choralist from Margaret Christy Davies. Choralist became the foundation bitch of the present-day Senjisfinx Basenjis. Through the years this kennel has produced very sound, typey Basenjis; the latest Champion to gain her title, in 1991, is Senjifinx Sulamix, a tricolour. In 1973 Karin Gabrielson imported Azenda Full Of It, and then Basenjis began to hit the high spots in Sweden. 'Loffe', as he was called, was a super show dog and won several Best in Groups, but the first, and so far the only Basenji to win Best in Show in Sweden was Sweet Conclusion of Dormtiki Azenda in 1976.

In 1977 three St Erme Basenjis, bred by Mirrie Cardew, were imported by three new

*Int. N. Ch.
Azenda Islanda:
Nordic winner
1979 and 1985.*

enthusiasts: Lars Malmquist (Madingo kennels), Staffen Drangen, and Kris Sandelberg (Beldam kennels). Lars Malmquist bought St Erme Legs Diamond, a Ch. Taysenji Yoko grandson. Legs was the first black and white in Sweden and is the ancestor of most of the black/whites in the country. Although, sadly, Lars Malmquist and Kris Sandelberg died prematurely, their dogs are still contributing to the breed. At the present time there are imports from Bokoto (Horners), Allandy (Mrs Allan), Jisgard (Gray), and Azenda (Christy Davies) which should fit in well with the Swedish breeding programme.

The Top Winning Swedish Basenjis are:

1. Int. Nordic Ch. Azenda Full Of It.
2. S. N. Ch. Sweet Conclusion of Dormtiki Azenda.
3. Int. N. Ch. Azenda Islanda, Nordic Winner 1979 and 1985, owned by Mia Lowbeer and Monica Massih.
4. Int. Nordic Ch. Senjifinx Kamonilla – the only Basenji to win the Swedish Basenji Society Specialty three times. She won her last BOB at the age of ten.
5. Int. Nordic Ch. N'Goros Azizi.
6. Int. Nordic Ch. N'Gashi Azenda.
7. S. N. Ch. Wamba's N'Wanaki.
(the last two both being placed in BIS finals in 1991).
8. Int. Nordic Ch. Senjisfinx Ismail – a top winning dog and producer with more than ten Champions to his credit.

Int. N. Ch.
Black Fula
Dandy of the
Congo.

NORWAY

In the sixties Pamela Steineger imported Black Fula Dandy and M'Boi of the Congo (a great grandson of the brindle S.A. Rhod. Ch. Binza of Laughing Brook) to her Rossanty Kennels. Unfortunately all these old bloodlines died out during the sixties and seventies when interest in the breed waned. It wasn't until 1986 that Basenjis were registered again, and dogs imported from Sweden began to figure in top placings at shows – with Nina Modahl's (Watzikima) Int. N. S. Ch. Nord. W-87 Tahzu's Red Rosebud, Liv Boe's (Shantari) Nord. Ch. Senjisfinx Nefertari, and Mr and Mrs Bonner's (Egypten) Int. Nord. Ch. Adonis all being placed in the Group at International and National shows.

In 1989 at the Swedish Basenji Society Specialty Show, judged by Robert Cole from Canada, Tahzu's Red Rosebud was Best in Show. New stock was required to increase the gene pool so enthusiasts imported dogs from England, mostly Azenda breeding, and a tricolour bitch from Finland, N. Ch. Gyltholmen's Favorita. These dogs have done a great deal for present-day stock in Norway; registrations have risen from nil in the early part of the eighties to 17 in 1991, and to 22 in 1992. The Basenji population has increased to around 80 dogs, with many more being shown. Although the breed is still considered rare, several of the imported dogs and their descendants have been placed in Groups at home and abroad, and interest in the breed is growing.

Amongst the latest imports are Charles Langaker's Domewood Cock O' The North, and a

Int. N. S. Ch. Azenda Gull: Norway's first Group winner.

bitch from Tenki breeding, from Mrs E. Grayson. Vidar Jacobsen's import Int. N. S. Ch. Azenda Gull was the first Basenji in Norway to win a Group – this was achieved at the International Show held by the Norwegian Kennel Club in June 1991. There is as yet no Norwegian Basenji Club – many owners are members of the Swedish Club – but in time the Norwegians may form their own club. Although the cold snowy climate of Scandinavia seems vastly different to their native habitat, the dogs appear to flourish there. Vidar Jacobsen writes that "In spite of a hard climate, Basenjis are well adapted to our conditions. They really love the snow, it seems harder for them to accept wind and rain (especially in combination)."

DENMARK
Pia Wright took Fallohide Dreamer and Galadriel, Golden Evenstar and a black/white bitch, Ellendil, with her in 1976 when she left England to live in Denmark. The following year she imported, from England, a grandson of Aus. Ch. Touch O'Class of Woz, Azenda Phuma. Phuma was campaigned throughout Europe, gaining many honours and putting Basenjis firmly on the map with regard to European Shows. A partnership with Susan Coe of Akuaba Kennels in America proved very successful, with the arrival on the Scandinavian and European scene of Am. Ch. Akuaba Bedevilled. 'Mickey Mouse' became the sire of several European litters, as well as excelling in the show ring. Like Norway, Denmark does not have a Basenji Club, but enthusiasm for the breed is increasing with many new owners and exhibitors becoming interested in the breed.

ITALY
Basenjis have been in Italy at least since 1966 when Mr and Mrs Sellers imported Yodeller of the Congo. He was followed in 1968 by Fula Dreamy and Fula Black Sprite of the Congo, bought

Int. It. Ch. Arabella Azenda: Hound Group winner in Monaco.

by Mr and Mrs L. Borletti. In the same year Miss Phyllis Cook sent out Riviana Black But Bonny and Riviana St Pauli's Girl to the CNEN Labatorio Radiobiologia Animale SSN Casaccia, while Topani Chiki Wonder went to Dr V. Moraco. The next recorded exports from the UK are a Houndsmark dog from Mollie Field, Horatio, to the Borlettis, and Jack Fleming's Shadow of Niangara to Mr D.G.Deignel in 1978. The following year two St Erme Basenjis, Black Arrow and Gay Pony, went to Dr P. C. Frabboni.

Int. It. Ch. Arabella Azenda, owned by Mrs G. Borletti, bred by Margaret Christie Davies, won the Hound Group at the Monaco Show in the early seventies. In 1980 St Erme Dancing Tarragon went to Mrs G. Borletti followed in 1984 by Azenda Free Style. In 1987 Nicola Salvadori exported Starshine at Pulcinella to Miss M. Ceccarelli, who handled her to her Italian title. There do not appear to be any further Italian imports until Catherine Wright's Dassita Satis went to Dardanio Manuli in Milan in 1990, and a Chaanrose dog from Rosie Lane went to Marco Servadi. At the present time there is not a Basenji Club in Italy, but there are plans afoot to create one.

SWITZERLAND

Basenjis have never really become popular in Switzerland, which is surprising when one considers the many qualities they possess. In 1958 Miss Helen N. Frey of Rumlang imported Branvil Sugar Kandi, a male, bred by Mrs I. Fox and a Gooses bitch bred by Colette Campbell. It appears that Mrs Frey intended to breed these two but never did. She found them "stubborn, disobedient and too prone to go off hunting. When free they did entirely as they wished, paid no heed to any call, returned when it suited them to do so, and were incredibly difficult to train."

In 1960 Mr N. Rothlisberger of Langnau bred his Dutch-born bitch, Verklikker, to Sugar Kandi. The resulting five red/white puppies are the only known litter to have been born in

Switzerland. Three more 'of the Congo' Basenjis arrived in the late fifties, and in 1961, and a St Erme bitch, Pony Carnival, in 1973, but nothing more is recorded regarding these animals. At the present time there are one or two Basenjis in the country being kept purely as pets.

FRANCE

Probably the best known Basenji breeder in France was Madame Rundle of St Martin du Var, who at one time had an extensive kennel. In 1974 the World Show was held in Paris, and there were fourteen Basenjis entered. The winning dog and Best of Breed was Vizir D'Iwor D'Antep, bred by M. Castanier; second place went to Voila Mister Speaker D'Alverne, bred by Mrs Rundle and owned by Madame Desschans; third place was Hengist of Houndsmark, owned by Lt and Mrs Wood from Germany; and in fourth place was Fula Kenge of the Congo, owned by Erna de Reus from Holland. Bitch winner and Best Opposite Sex was Kachina Pinta, bred by the Woods and owned by George Martin, West Germany; second place went to Sherry of Pine Crest, bred in the United States by Dean Guess and owned by Mr and Mrs McNeill, West Germany; third place went to Lionslair Fula Black Swan of the Congo, owned by the Woods; Fula Furore of the Congo, belonging to Erna de Reus, was fourth.

In the late sixties Mrs Rundle imported Tawny Simba from Mrs Drake in England. Mrs Rundle exhibited the dog at shows all over the Continent doing a great deal to advertise the breed, as many judges had never seen a Basenji in the flesh before his arrival in the show ring. At the present time an American-bred dog, Am. Ch. Edgie's Buckeye Traveller, owned by J. C. Edgerton and Hamoud and D. Miller, is being campaigned in France, winning Best of Breed, Best Dog of the Day and Reserve Best in Show at the International Beauvais Show 1991. This was followed by another Reserve Best in Show at Nantes, handled by Pierre Boetsch.

GERMANY

Houndsmark Hengist (a tricolour), bred by Mollie Field, and St Erme Dancing Pony were the two Basenjis that introduced the breed to Germany in 1973. Owned by an American couple, Mr and Mrs K. Wood (ex American Army), they were also the first of the breed to be shown in Hungary, winning CACIBs in 1974. Am. Ch. Kukuk's Harvey Wallbanger was imported by the Woods in 1975 as a useful outcross stud for Continental breeders. From 1972, when only two Basenjis were registered in the country, the number rose to more than thirty in 1975, due in the main to the Woods' enthusiasm for the breed. Berta Burkett, president of the German Basenji Club, founded her kennels on Ganymedes, a Basenji dog which she found as a stray. More recently there has been an influx of Basenjis imported from the United States and the UK. Among these is the black and white, Int. Lux. VDH Lucky Son of Woz, bred by Cecilia Wozniak and owned by Hoffman-Goetschke, who won Best of Breed at the 1990 World Show held in Dortmund. In Germany, as with other European countries, enthusiasm for the breed is on the increase.

HOLLAND

The first Basenji in Holland was owned by Jonkheer Van Sandbergh. On seeing a photograph of the Jonkheer with his dog, Erna de Reus determined to own a Basenji one day. In 1972 Erna bought Fula Furore and Fula Kenge of the Congo. Unfortunately these dogs were not suitable for breeding purposes, so her Basiateck's Kennel are founded on Riviana dogs, Rasjilah and Riviana Golden Fula of the Congo. In 1991 her multi Champion, Basiateck's Dark Kayola, won Best

*Multi Ch.
Basiateck's Dark
Kayola.*

*Queen Juliana
with Fula N'Zara
of the Congo.*

Opposite Sex at the World Show held in Germany. Miss de Reus is a consistent and successful exhibitor at most European shows. Arrianne Van Eeden Van Elk also has a successful kennel; her foundation stock is based on Azenda breeding.

It appears that most Dutch Basenji owners value their dogs for their companionship rather than their show potential, as, although show entries are small, Basenji social events produce a good number of dogs and owners. A good percentage of puppies born in the country are sold to owners in France or Germany. Possibly the best-known Basenji owner in Holland was the former Queen Juliana, who owned Fula N'Zara of the Congo. Zara is depicted sitting on the Queen Juliana's knee in the portrait given to the Queen by the People of Holland on the occasion of her Silver Jubilee. Other members of European Royal Houses to have owned Basenjis are Queen Helen, Queen Mother of Romania with Royal Tan of the Congo; King Michael and Queen Anne of Rumania, who possessed two Basenjis in the early sixties; and HSH The Princess Antoinette of Monaco, who also owned two dogs at one time.

IRELAND
Possibly the best-known Basenji kennels in Ireland were Syngefield, owned by Mr and Mrs J. R. Williams and situated at Birr in County Offaly. The Williams bred Basenjis successfully from the time Eng. Ir. Ch. Hercules of Syngefield was registered at the English Kennel Club in 1946 to 1959 when Genius of Syngefield was their final registration. Such well-known names spring to mind as Pluto and Artemis, both dual Champions, and Eng. Ir. Ch. Leda of Syngefield, the winner of a Best in Show in Ireland in the early fifties. Another important stud dog who contributed a great deal to the breed in the early days, was Eng. Ir. Ch. Syngefield Leonato of Littlebreach, bred by Mrs Percival, but sired by that other famous resident of the Syngefield kennels, Am. Ch. Kingolo. As well as importing Kingolo from America in order to offer new blood and genes to English and Irish breeders, many Syngefield-bred dogs crossed the Atlantic to America and made their mark over there. One of the best-known was Am. Ch. Brahme of Syngefield, owned by Mrs Belmont Ward's Bettina kennels.

During the years 1947 to 1949 Mrs Lewarn registered three dogs with the English Kennel Club – Specky of Thomastown, followed by Ch. Alderney of Thomastown, and his brother Guernsey of Thomastown. From the early fifties there appears to have been very little Basenji activity in the Irish show scene, until in 1973 Ros Loange bought Makindu Simona Loange, bred by Anne Forse. Two years later Mrs Loange thought she would like to breed a litter, but there were no Basenji males in Ireland at that time. Margaret Christy Davies sent over Zapotec Cucuracha, bred by Mrs Coutts, who sired a litter two days after arriving in Ireland. He was then eight months old! The following year Azenda High Dive went to Mrs St George Smith, of the Drumshallon Basenjis, and in 1977 Miss Christy Davies sent Azenda Red Sheen to her. In 1978 Red Sheen became the first Irish Basenji Champion since Leonato won his title more than twenty years earlier. Ir. Ch. Azenda Red Sheen has the honour of being the only Basenji to win an Irish Sporting Group. Anne Caffrey, of the Brookville Basenjis, sold Ir. Ch. Brookville Beauty to Mrs Mollie O'Driscoll. When Beauty was mated to Drumshallon Phantom in 1982 she produced three red, and three tricolour puppies. One of these, Bellini, made the journey back to England, and in the ownership of Mr and Mrs Richard Avis, he became the 180th English Champion.

The Championship system in Ireland differs from the British system. In order to achieve Championship status, a dog has to win forty points at Championship Shows where Green Stars are on offer for the breed. Green Stars have a certain points value, and they are awarded to the Best Dog and/or Bitch. The number of points available depend on how many dogs of the breed are actually present in the ring, plus a percentage calculation on how many were present at the same show the previous year. In actual fact, the winner is never certain of the exact number of points gained until the official confirmation arrives from the Irish Kennel Club. In the final total of forty Green Stars, the dog must have won two ten-point majors, or four five-point majors. If a

Eng. Ir. Ch.
Artemis of
Syngefield.

Fall.

Syngefield Ajax,
Syngefield Antea
and Int. Ch.
Syngefield
Artemis.

Fall.

Ch. Bellini: the 180th English Champion.

Dalton.

Ir. Ch. Azenda Red Sheen.

dog wins the Group, the points total won by the highest-placed beaten dog, is substituted for the number of breed points won by the winner.

In recent years, several British dogs have made the journey to Ireland, adding Irish Champion to their names, such as: Eng. Ir. Ch. Horsleys Sir Kincaid, Eng. Ir. Ch. Domewood Donner (bred by Bunty Bowers and owned by Marvin and Sally Wallis), Jane Gostynska's Eng. Ir. Champions Bubas Brown Bomber, Bubas Bombardier (bred by Joan Anderson) and Lavren Lord Lieutenant (bred by Liz Nerval). Present-day breeders on the island include: Mr and Mrs Finnigan, Mr Griffin (Szechwan) with dogs from Tabaqui, Adoram and Sepele, and Mrs I. E. Welch (Tallensi), who bought Ir. Ch. Tabaqui Santuzza of Bacchante from Kenny Stevenson as her foundation bitch. The Sheepham affix of Mr O'Donovan used Bredand dogs originally, as did Miss Hegarty, who has several Irish Champions to her credit, including My Black Metro, owned by Shirley Nicholson and handled to his title by Penny Reeves.

BERMUDA
The first Basenji ever to appear in the show ring in Bermuda was Am. Ch. Miacor's Zuchil, in 1959.

BARBADOS
Dr R. E. Nash introduced Basenjis to the island in 1971 when he bought Azenda Fula Forethought from Miss Christy Davies. At the present time Mr W. Welsh owns Basenjis imported from England, and these include Adoram Isna, Zizunga Willothwisp and Daneriver Catch a Star, all of which are consistent winners at the island shows.

HAWAII
Lyle and Helen Vaughan began their Koko Crater Basenji kennel in Honolulu in 1940 when they made a trip to the United States with the intention of buying Dobermans. Mrs Vaughan saw Kindu, Kasenyi and a puppy in California, fell in love with them, and they bought the three for $300 and took them back to Hawaii.

From then on, the Vaughans consistently bred good-coloured, typey, Basenjis for a decade until they hit the jackpot in 1956, when, at the Maui Kennel Club's All Breeds Show at Kalului Fairground, on 13th October, Philo's Blaze of Koko Crater went Best in Show under judge Forrest M. Hall, becoming the first American-bred Basenji to achieve this honour. Blaze was owned by Lt and Mrs Albert J. Ashurst of Pearl Harbour, but was handled to his win by Lyle Vaughan. Sadly, when Mr Vaughan died in 1957, the kennels had to be disbanded and most of the stock was sold.

Rex Tanaka of Honolulu, a keen Obedience enthusiast, trained Ch. Il-Se-Ott Golden Majorette to UDT in 1967, the first Basenji to hold a show Championship and a Tracking Dog title. In 1970 Mr Tanaka imported Fula Fair Lady of the Congo and Tenki's Fula Aquarius Azenda, bred by the Misses Juniper from England. 'Lady' obtained her Companion Dog Certificate, and 'Aquarius' went on to become Ch. Tenki's Fula Aquarius UTD – only the second Basenji to achieve this honour. Mr Tanaka has chosen 'Aquarius' as his kennel prefix. The No Ka Oi kennels, belonging to Rita L. Webb are also contributing to the breed.

JAPAN
In 1960, an article in the Japanese *Dog World* mentioned that a litter of eight Basenjis from American-registered parents, Hollywell Sammi (tricolour) and Cambria's Yoola, owned by Col and Mrs Ralph J. Schuctz, had been born in Yokohama. It is possible that one of the puppies was presented to the Crown Prince; the litter certainly appeared on Japanese television. It is recorded that 24 Basenjis were registered in Japan in 1990.

Chapter Ten

BREEDING BASENJIS

BREEDING PROGRAMMES

In simple language, without going into specific details of genes and chromosomes, breeders usually follow three lines with a breeding programme.

LINE BREEDING is the mating of individuals related by family lines to an outstanding ancestor, featured in both pedigrees.

IN BREEDING is the mating of closely related animals – mother to son, father to daughter, or brother to sister.

OUT CROSS BREEDING is the mating of an animal to one with a completely different pedigree, although with Basenjis, which have such a restricted gene pool, there are really no unrelated dogs.

The number of puppies in a litter is determined at the time of mating by the number of eggs (ova) the bitch has released, and the eventual number that are fertilised by the sperm and implanted into the uterus. Not all those that are implanted will go to full term; some may be aborted or absorbed. The number of ova a bitch releases may diminish with age. Ova are not manufactured by the bitch at each season. All the ova she will ever have are stored in her ovaries. Ova are not all discharged simultaneously; they are released over a period of days.

The male is responsible for the number of eggs fertilised as well as the sex of the offspring. As with humans, this is quite outside the control of the female. The conformation, colour, balance and type of a puppy are all imprinted at the moment of conception. Good or bad management and rearing can affect the final development of the dog, but they cannot change the original blueprint.

When breeding for colour:

RED TO RED will produce an all red litter, unless both animals carry the recessive tricolour gene, in which case one or more tricolour puppies may result. A tricolour in a litter from a red to red mating may come as a complete surprise to a breeder, especially if, on examination of the pedigrees, the only tricolour ancestors are seven or eight generations back.

RED TO TRICOLOUR will result in all reds unless the red parent carries the tri gene as above. A percentage of the resulting red puppies will carry the tri gene.

BLACK TO RED will give reds, blacks, and again, tricolours may appear if the recessive gene is carried by both parents. Black is a dominant colour and must be present in one parent to ensure black progeny. It is also possible that this mating could result in no black offspring.

BLACK TO TRICOLOUR will probably result in all three colours again, depending on the genes carried by the black parent.

BLACK TO BLACK – it is possible that this will again result in all three colours, depending on the colour of the parents' ancestors.

TRICOLOUR TO TRICOLOUR – the puppies are always tricolour. Recessive blacks can turn up in any litter where both parents carry that particular gene.

BRINDLE is a dominant colour and must be present in one parent, but again, it is possible that a brindle will not be produced in the resulting litter. As the brindle colour is only present in the United States at the moment, the full potential for the colour has still to be investigated and assessed.

THE BROOD BITCH

Ideally, before embarking on a breeding programme, three factors should be taken into consideration. Firstly, the bitch should be healthy, of good type and temperament, and should possess some good breed points to contribute to her future offspring. Secondly, there should be firm bookings for some, if not all of the proposed puppies to suitable homes. Thirdly, and maybe most importantly, you should have the facilities to whelp and rear a litter, and 'to run on' any puppies that are not sold, and take back any whose new owners have proved unsuitable to care for a Basenji. It cannot be stressed too strongly that the Basenji is not a "commercial" breed. They will not fit into all lifestyles, so great care must be taken when selling the puppies. They should go to owners who understand all the bad as well as the good points about the breed.

Never, ever, be tempted to breed a litter just "for the good of the bitch." Equally, "letting the bitch have a litter" will not prevent future false pregnancies, if the bitch was formerly prone to that condition. Bitches can live long, healthy lives without ever having been mothers, and a pregnancy will not cure a false pregnancy problem; it is much more likely to make future false pregnancies even worse.

Make a careful study of dogs and pedigrees in an effort to find a stud dog that will complement the bitch, looking for compatible bloodlines and sound temperament. Never breed from dogs with uncertain tempers; that trait is almost certain to be inherited and passed on down future generations. Once the stud dog has been selected, contact the owner to arrange such matters as stud fee, pick of litter, and any other details which, if overlooked at this time, can ruin any transaction and friendship.

Basenjis normally come into season once a year, around September/October. Whatever the country, Basenji litters appear to be born mostly during the winter months. My imported American bitch had to change her season to accommodate the African winter in April, June, and July, and then she had to revert again to September/October when we returned to the UK.

Very occasionally, a puppy may have a season when it is only four or six months old, but, of course, she should never be bred from at this age. If a bitch has pups at her first season, before she has finished maturing, she will be utilising essential nutrients and calcium for her puppies that are still necessary for her own well-being. It is better to wait until the bitch is two or three years old before contemplating having a litter from her.

Sometimes a Basenji will come into season during the summer months. As far as the breeder is concerned, this is a lovely time to have puppies; they can be put out to play in the warm sunshine and life is altogether easier. However, it is not always possible to persuade the stud dog that he has a duty to perform at this time. In fact, when Basenjis first came into England, it was said that the dogs also had a season in the autumn and would only mate a bitch at this time. One thing is certain – Basenji dogs always seem to know the mating season. Owners who keep one or more males as house dogs all say that around September/October the dogs' temperaments will change. They become edgy; tempers fray and fights are never far away.

It is generally assumed that a bitch is ready for mating at the tenth to fourteenth day from the onset of her season, i.e. when the ova are released to accept the sperm. But be warned – a Basenji is a Basenji, and many of them have other ideas about the subject. On average, a Basenji's season lasts longer than other breeds, sometimes extending to four or even five weeks, instead of the usual three week period.

The optimum day for conception may also vary widely. For instance, some bitches are fertile as early as the third or fourth day, while the native-born Amatangazig of the Congo did not ovulate until the twentieth day. I once had a bitch who, having been mated at great expense on what I thought was her correct day – the twelfth – spent the whole of her twenty-fourth day of the season teaching a young five-month-old male the facts of life. She succeeded as well, and those were the puppies that arrived sixty-three days later! That particular bitch was a puppy lover; she was even known to kidnap and produce milk for her daughter's babies!

Sometimes a female can be non-maternal, but this type is rare, as most Basenjis make excellent, even protective mothers. My American tricolour, Ch. Asaris Ti Karu, was definitely one of the non-maternal kind. I missed mating her at the first season because she swore at her prospective mate so much that I felt sure that a mistake had been made with regard to the correct day. On the next season she was mated – her language was unbelievable – but the deed was done.

Pregnancy proceeded normally, and the puppies arrived without undue fuss. She fed them, cleaned them, and then left them! For the next three weeks this pattern continued until I gave the puppies their first taste of meat. She then handed over all her responsibilities to me, only standing to give them milk on my insistence. Little wonder that her figure returned to normal so quickly that she was able to take Best of Breed at Crufts with a litter of seven-week-old puppies at home! At the other end of the scale, there are those females for whom the third or fourth day is the correct time for mating, so it is largely a case of trial and error. A good, steady stud dog is always a great help; he will almost certainly know the correct day!

THE MATING

Take the bitch to the stud on the day you think she is ready. Don't rush things; give the dogs the opportunity to play and relieve themselves in an enclosed space. If the bitch flirts with the dog by turning her vulva towards him and switching her tail to one side, she will probably accept him when he mounts her. If, on the other hand, she consistently turns on the dog and he is not really persistent, then there has probably been a mistake with the timing, and the visit should be repeated a day or two later. It is possible to ask the vet take a swab in order to ascertain if the bitch is ovulating and when would be the optimum time for the mating, but this is not always feasible.

After the stud has mated the bitch, he will turn himself round so that they are standing end to end while they are 'tied'. The tie occurs because the section of the dog's penis just behind the penis bone is filled with blood and swells to almost three times its normal size, so it cannot be withdrawn from the bitch until the swelling subsides. The time a tie can last varies from five minutes to sixty minutes. For many generations and thousands of years, dogs have performed this perfectly natural act without human assistance.

However, in these modern times, it is considered advisable to have one person holding the head of the bitch, and another holding the dog in order to prevent any accidental injury while the pair are tied. It is therefore essential to arrange for the mating to take place inside, in the warmth. Sitting on damp grass on a cold day for sixty minutes, with a comparative stranger at the other end of two dogs is really not to be recommended! Some breeders like to repeat the mating on the second day, though, personally, I have never found this necessary – one mating always seems to be enough with a misalliance! A word of warning here, Basenji bitches are always *very* vocal during the act, especially maidens. It is only the true nymphomaniacs and the truly maternal types that appear to enjoy the experience.

THE PREGNANCY
Some females give early indication that they are carrying puppies; they will become more sedate, and their teats become pink in colour. A few even have morning sickness, and there can be faddiness over food, or, alternatively, the bitch may have a ravenous appetite and start eating for ten straightaway! Around four to five weeks there should be definite signs of pregnancy: teats become larger, there is a broadening across the loin, and there is a swelling of the stomach. If there is any doubt that the bitch is in whelp by the sixth week, then there is a strong possibility that she has 'missed'. The bitch can have an ultrasound scan at three weeks to confirm pregnancy and the number of whelps that are expected. Some breeders have the ability to feel puppies and count embryos as hard little lumps in the womb at the same age, but generally most people just wait until the due date, or try to count the pups as they kick the dam's stomach during her relaxed periods when she is asleep in front of the fire.

At five to six weeks the prospective mother's food intake should be increased, to almost double the usual amount, but this should be split into two meals so that the stomach does not become over-extended and become more uncomfortable than it would be normally. At seven weeks the same amount of food should be divided into three meals. Do not let the bitch get fat and flabby; she must have ample, gentle exercise to keep her muscles in trim for the labour ahead. It is a good idea to accustom the bitch to the whelping box by placing it in her sleeping quarters. The most suitable whelping box is wooden, with 'pig bars' placed along the back and sides to provide a safe haven for puppies, should they be in danger of being squashed by the mother lying on them. Unless the outside temperature is very hot, extra heating will be required for the newborn puppies. This can be a low-heat electric pad, placed underneath the bedding, or an infra-red lamp placed over the box. In either case, check the wiring very carefully to make sure that it cannot be chewed by the mother or in the future by the puppies.

The normal temperature for a dog is 101.5 degrees Fahrenheit; twelve to eighteen hours before the bitch is due to whelp this can drop to 98F. If the temperature is taken daily for the last ten days of pregnancy, this decrease can provide some clue as to when the puppies may arrive. Most pregnancies last sixty-three days, although puppies can arrive up to five days early or late, without any ill effects. The early arrivals will probably be later in opening their eyes than those born on the sixty-third day. Similarly, those born later than the due date will be advanced in their development.

EQUIPMENT FOR WHELPING

As the whelping date approaches, place thick layers of newspaper in the whelping box and make sure that you have the following articles to hand:

A soft towel.
Flash light.
Sharp, rounded scissors.
Potassium permanganate crystals.
Disinfectant.
Plenty of clean newspaper.
A clean box, well padded and heated, to place newborn puppies in, if required.

THE WHELPING

Usually the first signs of imminent birth are frantic digging and tearing up of newspapers, which should have been placed in the whelping box, ready for nest-making. However, being a contrary female and a typical Basenji, she may scorn the man-made den and try to make her own nest in the best armchair, in a cupboard, or under a bed. This last choice should be firmly discouraged; it is not easy to give assistance during whelping while lying face-down under a bed! The first bitch I ever had, dropped her mongrel puppy on my chest while I was having a long lie in bed, one Sunday morning. She had given no sign of being in labour and had certainly not prepared a nest. At that time, neither she nor I knew anything about puppies.

In more conventional cases, the digging activity can continue for quite a while, and in-between times the bitch will demand to go out to relieve herself, and there may be periods of sleep. Eventually she will begin to strain, the contractions becoming stronger until a black water-bag becomes visible at the vulva. The bitch will usually break this, and within a short time – and three or four more strong contractions – the first puppy should arrive. If she is still straining after an hour, with no further sign of the puppy, contact the vet immediately. It has been known for a maiden bitch to drop her first puppy outside while she is on one of her many trips to relieve herself. This is the time that the flash-light comes into use! It is always a good idea to give the vet advance warning of a proposed litter, so that he will be prepared to give assistance if required.

A maiden bitch will possibly scream as the puppy emerges and become panic-stricken about what is happening to her. After all, it is a very painful and frightening experience. Restrain the bitch, and calm her down. It is more than likely that she will require assistance to remove the puppy from the amniotic sac. The whelp should not remain in the sac for more than thirty seconds, as it is important that it must start breathing as soon as possible. Once the pup is clear of the sac, cut the umbilical cord, if the bitch has not already severed it, leaving at least a centimetre attached to the puppy. Rub the puppy briskly with a towel to encourage breathing, and then give it to the mother to dry and clean. As the puppy is expelled it will be accompanied by fluid, some of which is bright-red, some dark-red, and some green. This colour is caused by an in-utero breakdown of certain tissues prior to whelping and it is not a cause for concern.

The normal birth presentation is head-first, with the head resting on the paws. Any deviation from this is a breech presentation, but serious breeches are not common with Basenjis. The vertex breech – when the forelegs are folded back under the chest – does not usually cause any difficulty, and neither does the bottom presentation. In both cases the breeder can assist by

After a puppy is born, instinct will lead it to suckle.

A Basenji bitch waiting for the next arrival.

A puppy at a day old.

Newborn puppies: note the colours.

holding the presented portion with a clean towel, and carefully extracting the rest of the animal at the next contraction.

The shoulder presentation – when the head is turned back on the body, while one leg and and shoulder are in the vulva – presents a far more serious problem. If a vet is not readily available, assistance can be given by inserting a well-lubricated index finger through the vulva into the pelvic inlet, then gently hooking the pup's jaw and pulling it towards the vulva. Once straightened, birth should continue normally, but veterinary help is imperative if there is any delay in delivery.

It is very probable that the bitch's reaction to all this pain will be to attack the hand that is helping her, so it is as well to have someone holding her head while the pup is being turned. Instinct is a wonderful thing; once the dam has delivered the first whelp she will clean and stimulate the puppy, and in no time at all the puppy will find the way to the milk-bar. The next contraction should expel the afterbirth; race memory will encourage the bitch to eat this, firstly as a source of food, for the time that she would be unable to leave the den to hunt, and, secondly, to remove any substance that might attract predators. A careful check must be kept to ensure that all afterbirths are expelled. If you are in any doubt, ask the vet to give the bitch an injection to contract her womb and expel anything that is left inside her.

As the puppies are born, check them over carefully, weigh them (the kitchen scales are adequate for this), record the colour, the markings and the sex. After the arrival of the first puppy, the dam will clean and nurse it until the next contraction, which is usually within thirty minutes or an hour at the most. This time the mother should be able to cope by herself, but do not leave her, just in case help is needed.

It is advisable to have a small cardboard box ready with a hot-water bottle under a blanket; the newborn puppies can be placed in this while subsequent puppies are being born. The dam will often move around without much thought for those already born, and she might possibly injure them. Return the pups to the dam as soon as is feasible, because she will be very anxious about them. Never take the box out of her sight. If subsequent puppies fail to appear after the birth of the first, in spite of an appreciable time of straining, contact a vet immediately. Never let the bitch labour in vain, without help.

A Basenji litter can contain any number from one to eight, the norm being three or four. After all the whelps have arrived, take the bitch out to relieve herself. It is very probable that she will be very unwilling to leave the babies, and she may have to be carried away. On her return, give a drink of milk or water, and then let her settle down with the puppies. While she is absent, use the opportunity to provide fresh, clean bedding. Check that all the puppies are warm and contented, and make sure that they have all fed. This first feed of colostrum, which is present in the first milk, contains all the dam's antibodies and these will give the pups immunity from infection during their first few weeks.

WHELPING COMPLICATIONS
There are two conditions that may affect the pregnant bitch. These are:

ECLAMPSIA: This is an insufficiency of the parathyroid glands, which causes a sudden lowering of the blood calcium level. This results in restlessness, rapid heart action, staggering, collapse and muscle cramps. An immediate calcium injection is required, as the condition can be fatal. Preventive feeding of a vitamin/calcium supplement during pregnancy is recommended.

UTERINE INERTIA
Primary inertia: This is the failure of the bitch to come into labour at term. This can be caused by poor muscle tone, excessive weight, or a degenerative uterus.
Secondary inertia: This is caused by exhaustion and it may occur during labour. The bitch will make no attempt to expel any remaining puppies. This is a case requiring veterinary assistance.

REMOVAL OF DEWCLAWS
Most Basenjis have the dewclaws removed from the front legs. These are the small claws situated on the inside of the leg, just above the pastern. They serve no useful purpose, although some breeders prefer to leave them on. Dewclaws on the back legs are almost unknown. Experienced breeders will do the simple operation of removing the dewclaws themselves, or a vet will perform the task when the pups are two to three days old. This can be a traumatic

experience for all concerned, as the dam will fret when the pups are removed to be treated.

I have always found that it is easy, painless and bloodless to attend to the puppies when they are newborn, dealing with each one in turn while the dam is occupied with cleaning the next arrival. Use a sharp pair of curved scissors, and make sure that you get below the joint – a quick nip and the job is done, leaving a very small scar that heals within two to three days. This way, there is no trauma for the pup or the mother. If the umbilical cord is nipped too close to the stomach wall, which may happen with enthusiastic and excitable bitches, a few grains of potassium permanganate crystals will contain the bleeding. The same applies if the dewclaws bleed when they are removed, although that is a very unlikely occurrence as there is very little blood in that area so soon after birth.

THE FIRST THREE WEEKS
First-time Basenji breeders may receive a considerable shock when they see the colour of the newborn puppies; they are mousey-coloured, ranging from light grey to almost black. Worry not, they will change colour within a few days. The very dark-coloured pups will have a dark-red adult coat, while the greys will be a lighter shade of red. Tricolours usually appear with tan markings in place, but occasionally the tan does not materialise for about a week, making you wonder just what the final colour will be. Fula Blacks can appear to be black and white at birth, but gradually, over the weeks, the tan hairs will appear. There is never any doubt with the blacks; they are jet-black from the beginning.

After all the excitement is over, leave the dam and puppies in peace for a couple of days, just checking that the puppies are feeding and that they are warm. A contented litter will make very little noise. If the puppies are constantly crying and whimpering, this is almost certainly an indication that all is not well. The pups may be too cold or too hot, or the supply of milk may not be up to standard. During this time, check on the bitch to see that she does not have an excessive discharge, and make sure that her mammary glands are not engorged, hard, or sore. If you notice anything untoward, call the vet immediately.

During the next three weeks there is little for the breeder to do, except to ensure that the whelping box is kept scrupulously clean, the bitch is fed and watered, and the babies are fat and contented. Once the puppies are born, I prefer to dispense with the newspaper bedding. Puppies cannot get a good grip on such a smooth surface, and Basenji pups are amazingly mobile even at such a young age. Bedding, whether it is towelling or a commercial product, should be affixed to the floor, otherwise there is danger of suffocation to a pup as the dam scratches the bedding up to make a more comfortable nest.

Puppies' nails grow fast at this stage; they become like little needles, and they can cause injury to the dam's mammary glands. They should, therefore, be cut back as far as possible – without cutting the quick – at least once a week. A sharp pair of scissors will do the job very easily. While the puppies are relatively immobile, the dam will attend to all their needs – 'topping and tailing' them – but Basenji babies are never really immobile. They are often up and moving long before their eyes open, at around the fifteenth day, so it is essential to have a raised front to the box to prevent them falling out.

WEANING
Weaning is the next step, and this is normally started at the fourth week. However, if it is a large litter, and the mother is losing condition because of the pups' healthy appetites, it is as well to

*Puppies
feeding at
four weeks.*

start after three weeks. Everybody has a different system of weaning – all of which appear to work equally well. Personally, I start by feeding each puppy a little taste of fresh mince (ground beef). Hold the pup in your hand, and offer it a small pinch of meat. As far as the the forward pups are concerned, a sniff is all that is required before the meat is snatched from your fingers.

The more backward pups may have to have the meat placed in their mouth. However, all they need is one taste, and the expression that comes over their faces is one of sheer delight and surprise. That piece of meat is gulped down, and they are snuffling around for more. The next day I feed a slightly larger helping of meat, and then I progress to mince mixed with well-soaked puppy meal, weetabix, porridge, rice or pasta, plus a teaspoon of natural yoghurt. I slowly increase the number of meals I feed, until by the fifth week the pups are getting four meals in twenty-four hours. Sample menus might be:

BREAKFAST: Porridge or cereal, mixed with milk (either cow's or a commercial, dried type).
LUNCH: Mince (ground, raw beef), plus well-soaked puppy meal and milk.
SUPPER: Sardines, rice, cooked or raw vegetables (chopped up), plus milk and a teaspoonful of natural yoghurt. *The yoghurt is a good preventative for puppy diarrhoea.*
NIGHT-TIME MEAL: Puppy meal and milk.

At the fourth week, change to cooked meat instead of raw. Alternate with a commercial canned food, and fish, sardines, pilchards or tuna. Add cooked vegetables to some of the meals – scrambled eggs are also popular. I do not advocate giving any extra vitamins; with a well varied diet there should be no need for supplements, and over-dosing, especially of calcium, can cause problems. If the future diet for the dog is to be an all-in-one food, this can be introduced at this stage, but do be sure to leave water available at all times. Water should always be accessible for the pups once they are weaned, but most particularly if you are feeding a dehydrated food.

During this period the bitch should be providing milk, but that source will gradually decrease, and by the sixth week – or a little sooner – the puppies should be entirely independent of their mother. However, they will still suckle if they get the chance, and some dams will let the puppies do this for a very long time. While the dam's milk supply is decreasing, there is a chance that she will regurgitate her food for the puppies. This action is perfectly normal, but it can be annoying for the breeder, as the pups – being true Basenjis – will never refuse food, and they may end up with very distended stomachs, thus increasing the chance of any incipient umbilical hernia enlarging.

Some breeders advocate feeding puppies from a communal tray, but I prefer to use individual bowls so that I know exactly how much each puppy has eaten. My aim is to send puppies to their new homes, at seven to eight weeks of age, well adapted to any type of food and ready to switch to the new owner's choice. Nowadays, worming is a comparatively simple operation. The first dose may be given as early as three weeks with a one-dose substance such as Panacur. This particular treatment has the advantage of removing any eggs that a bitch puppy may have acquired in its womb from its mother, thus ensuring that at some time in the future her own puppies will be born free of worms. Treatment should be repeated at six weeks.

HOUSE TRAINING
Basenjis are extremely easy to toilet train; they will instinctively move away from their bedding, retiring to the furthest corner of the box to relieve themselves. I prefer to use a cat litter tray rather than newspaper. The cat litter can get scattered around, especially when fresh and the puppies scrabble in it, but I think the advantages outweigh the disadvantages. Starting when the pups are three weeks old, they can be placed in the box on awakening and after they have fed, and within a very short time the feel of the litter beneath their feet will trigger off the correct response. As they become more active the box can be moved to the play area, and by the time they are six weeks old – apart from the odd accident – the pups will be using it as required.

READY TO LEAVE HOME
Eyes open around the fifteenth day, ears usually come up at five weeks, and tails begin to go over the back and curl at the same age. Tails may go on tightening and curling up to nine months when the final stage should be achieved. The pups should now be ready to go off to their new homes; they have been accustomed to a variety of foods, they have been wormed, they are used to being picked up gently by family and visitors and played with, they have heard noises like vacuum cleaners, radios and televisions, and they have explored their immediate surroundings. If the weather has been clement, the pups will have been outside for short periods; they will have worn soft cat collars in order to become used to the feel of a restriction round their necks. In short, they will have been made as independent and socialised as possible at such a young age.

Chapter Eleven

HEALTH CARE AND HEREDITARY CONDITIONS

Basenjis are normally very healthy, and hardly ever require a visit to the vet, except for inoculations and yearly boosters. However, Basenji owners should be aware some of the misfortunes that have been noted in the breed. The following is a layman's synopsis of some of these conditions.

ALLERGIES
These can be caused by many things: insect bites, stings, household products, grass pollen, and sometimes diet. Some Basenjis have yearly attacks of skin irritation that appears to be a canine form of hay fever. In all instances, the animal comes up in itchy lumps and bumps, suffering acute distress. Veterinary assistance is required immediately.

BLADDER STONES
Cystinuria Cystine is the substance formed as the result of the normal breakdown of some protein types by the body. In some Basenjis this cystine is not re-absorbed back into the body from urine by the kidneys as it should be, and builds up enough to form stones in the bladder. Not all bladder stones are of the same type. Veterinary advice must be sought.

DIABETES
A canine condition similar to that suffered by humans. Glucose is excreted in the urine and the blood, accompanied by increased water consumption and urination. Testing for glucose in the urine may be performed with the use of a diabetic test tape, available from most pharmacies. Treatment is by veterinary advice with the use of controlled injections of insulin.

EYES
Progressive Retinal Atrophy or PRA: This is a progressive degeneration of the retina, which is the sensory layer located at the back of the eye. As this layer degenerates or dies, vision is lost until total blindness results. Normally PRA cannot be detected until the animal is four or five years old.

Persistent Pupillary Membrane or PPM: This is present, to a greater or lesser degree, in the eyes of most Basenjis. During the last few weeks of gestation a membrane covers the eye. This membrane is composed of vessels that feed the iris, which later dissolves to become the pupil. The pupillary membrane is still present in puppies when their eyes open, and it can be seen quite clearly as a fine network in the pupillary area. Atrophy of the membrane should begin around three weeks of age, and be completed by five weeks. It is advisable to have all puppies eye-tested at eight weeks of age. In the mildest form, a few strands or tags may still be present; vision is not affected and the strands may disappear with age. In the severest form, strands may be associated with cataract. PPM can be caused environmentally by any interruption in the progress of a pregnancy or by illness in a puppy at a young age. It is interesting to note that PPM tags were found in half of the African-bred Basenjis taken to the United States in 1989.

FALSE PREGNANCY
This is a very common occurrence with Basenji females. About nine weeks from the time a bitch would have been fertile during her season, she will start nest-making and producing milk. In most cases, the bitch will return to normal in about three weeks, but occasionally the milk production will be heavy enough to require veterinary treatment to disperse it.

FANCONI SYNDROME (Renal Tubular Dysfunction)
This is a hereditary disorder of the kidney in man and dogs. Normally, electrolytes such as potassium, sodium and bicarbonate are recovered from body fluids and returned to the blood stream by the kidneys. In the case of Fanconi disease these essential substances are excreted in the urine.

In most cases the onset of the disease is not noted until the age of four or five, when increased water consumption and urination may be observed. Glucose is excreted in the urine – this may be tested for by using any of the human diabetic tests. Unlike diabetic sufferers, glucose is not present in the blood of the Fanconi victim. Treatment consists of replacing the missing amino acids, and this has proved to be of great value in extending the active life of the sufferer.

HAEMOLYTIC ANAEMIA
This is an inherited type of anaemia. It causes the red cells, that are manufactured by the bone marrow, to be deficient in an enzyme called pyruvate kinase. In normal circumstances, pyruvate kinase creates enough energy from the metabolizing of blood sugar for the red cells to carry out normal activities. The absence of pyruvate kinase means that the red cells lack energy, and die off quickly.

The bone marrow will replace the red cells more quickly than normal, but it cannot continue at this rate, and so eventually no more red cells are produced, resulting in death. Most HA afflicted animals die before two years of age. This condition was prevalent in the sixties, but by selected breeding and the exclusion of carriers, the incidence of the disease has declined until at the present time it is virtually unknown.

HYPOTHYROIDISM
The Basenji breed is unique in its thyroid function, having a more rapid thyroid turnover than any other breed of dog. The breed has a reputation for being a 'hyper' breed, possibly due to thyroid function.

IPSID (Immunoproliferative Small Intestinal Disease) This is also referred to a Mal-absorption. Dogs with IPSID often show signs of acute diarrhoea, loss of appetite and weight loss. These symptons are increased if the dog becomes unduly stressed. Boarding, vaccination, oestrus, pregnancy or major surgery have all been noted before the onset of the condition.

KENNEL COUGH
This is a highly infectious illness produced by Bordetella Bronchoseptica bacteria or Canine Parainfluenza virus. The disease is most usually contracted at shows, training clubs or boarding kennels. It can be a serious condition for very young puppies, or the elderly adult. The cough persists for about six weeks, but the dog carries the infection for about fourteen weeks. There are preventative vaccines available.

PYROMETRA
This is the accumulation of pus in the uterus caused by a bacteria such as staphylococcus, which gains entrance during the heat period or after whelping. It usually goes undetected until the bitch becomes ill and/or an abnormal discharge is noticed. This is a serious condition which may require a hysterectomy; it may result in death if not treated.

HERNIAS
UMBILICAL HERNIA Basenjis are prone to a weakening of the mid-line stomach muscle, allowing the intestine to protrude. In most cases this is a very minor defect which can be rectified by gently pushing back the protuberance during puppyhood. In very severe cases, or if the hernia is unsightly, a minor operation – when the puppy is six months old – may be required.
INQUINAL HERNIAS These are much less common, but far more serious, and must always be treated surgically. This condition was present in some of the early breeding stock, but by selective breeding and the elimination of carriers, is rarely seen at the present time.

WORMS
All puppies must be wormed at three and six weeks of age, and thereafter on a regular six-monthly basis.

EUTHANASIA
Unlike humans, dogs are granted the merciful kindness of euthanasia. When the inevitable time comes when the quality of a dog's life has diminished, either through illness or old age, it will be your responsibility to ensure that the dog is given a loving and peaceful end in the company of the person it knows best – you. Do not allow your dog to exist in bewilderment and pain because you cannot face the prospect of losing your companion – a dog deserves better than that after the love and pleasure it has given. A simple, painless injection of an anaesthetic overdose administered by a vet, ensures a peaceful, unstressful end.

APPENDICES

A SELECTION OF BASENJI BOOKS

Some books with African Basenji connections:

Im Herzen von Afrika, Dr Schweinfurth, 1918.
Among Congo Pygmies, Paul Schebesta. Published by Hutchinson Co, 1933.
My Pygmy and Negro Hosts, Paul Schebesta. Published by Hutchinson Co, 1936
Fabulous Congo, Felice Belloti. Published by Andrew Dakers Ltd, 1954.
Leopard in My Lap, Michaela Denis. Published by Julia Messner Inc, 1955.
Facing Danger in the Last Wilderness, Published by Bolton House Inc, 1962.
Congo Kitabu, Jean Pierre Hallet. Published by Random Press, 1966.
Land and People of the Kasai, Hilton Simpson.
Figures of Eight, Patricia Cockburn. Published by Chatto & Windus, Hogarth Press.

Basenji Books, now out of print, that have become collector's items:

Basenjis, The Barkless Dogs. Veronica Tudor Williams. Published by James Heap, 1946. ("The Red Book").
Basenjis, The Barkless Dogs, Veronica Tudor Williams. Published by Whatmoughs Ltd, 1954, and 2nd Edition revised with different photographs 1954. ("The Blue Book").
Basenjis, The Barkless Dogs, Veronica Tudor Williams. Published by David & Charles, 1976.
Fula, Basenji from the Jungle, Veronica Tudor Williams. Published privately, 1988.
Basenji – Dog from the Past, Forrest B. Johnson. Published privately, 1978.
Call of the Marsh, Jill Wyllie. Books of Rhodesia, 1979 (True story).
Canis Basenji, Robert Vavra. Published by the Basenji Club of America, 1958 (Cartoons).
A Donkey and a Dandelion, Doris Rybot. Published by Hutchinson, 1966 (Fiction).

Chad, A. Stephen Tring. Reindeer Books, 1966 (Children's Fiction).
Goodbye My Lady, James Street. Published by The People's Book Club, 1941 (Fiction).
Weep no more, My Lady, James Street. *Saturday Evening Post* Dec 6th 1941. (Fiction)
The Basenji Illustrated, Robert Cole. Published privately, 1978.

Basenji Books still available:

A Basenji for Me, Mirrie St Erme Cardew. Published by Midland Counties, 2nd ed.1986.
Your Basenji, Evelyn M. Green. Denlingers Pub. Ltd, 1976.
How to Raise and Train a Basenji Jack Schafer and Bob Mankey. TFH Publications Inc,1966.
The Basenji – Out of Africa to You, Susan Coe. Doral Publishing, 1990.
The Basenji Stacked and Moving, Robert Cole. Cole Book Imprint, 1987.
Candle, Ann Smith. Doral Pub. Co 1991 (A child's Christmas story).

Basenji Champion and Pedigree Books:

Basenji Champions:1937/77, J. W. Stringer and E. M. Ford. Published privately, 1978.
Basenji Champions:1979/89, J. W. Stringer. Published privately, 1991.
Basenji Champions: 1945/81, Staff of Jan Linday Freund. Camino E. E. & B. Co, 1982.
Basenji Champions: 1982/86, Jan Bruner. Camino E. E. & B. Co, 1988.
T*he Years of the American Basenji,* M. Russell and S. Coe. Published privately, 1980, with yearly updates.
*Finnish Champion/Pedigree Boo*k. 1991. Finnish Basenji Club.
The Basenji (A/Asia) Hound Assoc. N.S.W. & Basenji Club of Victoria. 1947/76.
The Basenji (A/Asia) Hound Association N.S.W. 1976/81.
The Basenji (A/Asia) Hound Association N.S.W. 1981/89.
Basenji Magazine.
The Basenji Monthly, Susan Coe, 89 Linton Hill Road, Newtown PA 18940.

NATIONAL KENNEL CLUBS AND BREED CLUBS

UNITED KINGDOM

The Kennel Club,
1 Clarges Street,
Piccadllly, London WlA 8AB

The Basenji Club Of Great Britain,
Hon. Sec. Mrs I. Terry,
13 Rennets Close,
Eltham, London SE9 2LG.

Basenji Owners and Breeders Association,
Hon. Sec. Mrs E. N. Ford,
46 South Street,
Partridge Green,
West Sussex RH13 8EL.

The Northern Basenji Society,
Hon. Sec. Mrs A. Broadbent,
89 Acres Hall,
Pudsey, Leeds,
West Yorkshire LS28 9DY.

IRELAND.

The Irish Kennel Club Ltd,
Fottrell House, Unit 6,
Greenmount Office Park,
Dublin 6 W. (Harold's Cross Bridge).

UNITED STATES OF AMERICA

The American Kennel Club,
51 Madison Avenue,
New York, N.Y 10010.

The Basenji Club Of America,
Secretary Susan Patterson Ward,
2973 Dogwood Court,
Bremen, Indiana 46506.

There are 18 State Basenji Clubs affiliated to the BCOA.

CANADA

The Canadian Kennel Club,
89 Skyway Avenue,
Etobicoke,
Ontario M9W 6R4.

Basenji Club Of Canada,
Sec. Christine Kemster,
3452 Dubrobin Road,
RR3
Woodlawn, ON KOA 3MO,
Canada.

SCANDINAVIA

Finnish Basenji Club,
Lella Karkas,
Arvinkatu 8B4,
20100 Turku,
Finland.

Swedish Basenji Club,
Mia Lowbeer,
Arkov 25,
S-12155 Johanneshov,
Sweden.

AUSTRALIA

Australia National Kennel Council,
Royal Show Grounds,
Ascot Vale,
Victoria,
Australia.

Basenji Club New South Wales,
Sec. Trevor Robb,
P.O.Box 68,
Albion Park,
New South Wales 2527
Australia.

Basenji Club Of Victoria,
c/o Mrs Doreen Durrin,
160 Warrandyte Road,
Ringwood,
Victoria 3134,
Australia.

AFRICA

Kennel Union Of Southern Africa,
6th Floor, Bree Castle,
68 Bree Street,
Cape Town 8001,
Rep. South Africa.

636.753   Ford, Elspet.
F
          The complete
          Basenji.

DATE			